D0922644

PAINTING ◦ COLOR ◦ HISTORY

COLLECTION PLANNED AND DIRECTED BY
ALBERT SKIRA

GOYA

THE FRESCOS IN
SAN ANTONIO DE LA FLORIDA
IN MADRID

HISTORICAL AND CRITICAL STUDY BY
ENRIQUE LAFUENTE FERRARI

Francisco José de Goya y Lucientes

PUBLISHED UNDER THE PATRONAGE
OF THE ROYAL ACADEMY OF FINE ARTS
OF SAN FERNANDO

ALBERT SKIRA PUBLISHER

TRANSLATED BY STUART GILBERT

PHOTOGRAPHS BY HANS HINZ, BASEL · PLATES ENGRAVED BY GUEZELLE ET RENOUARD, PARIS

Published by Skira Inc., Publishers, New York, N.Y. Library of Congress Catalog Card Number 55-10595.

Printed in Switzerland

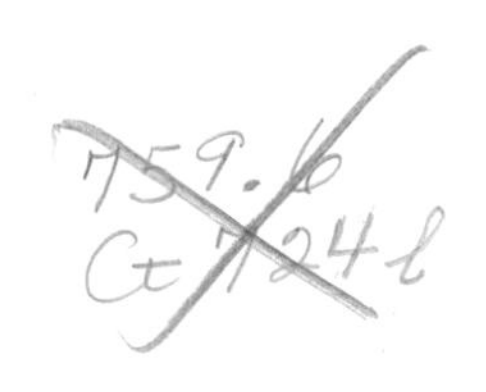

We are particularly appreciative of the honor done us by the Royal Academy of San Fernando in authorizing us to make this book, in which for the first time the public can see, reproduced in all their splendor, the frescos in the church of San Antonio de la Florida in Madrid. Our thanks are due to Don Fernando Alvarez de Sotomayor, director of the Academy of San Fernando, Madrid; to Don José Francés, perpetual secretary of the Academy; to Don José Yarnoz Larrosa, treasurer of the Academy; to the Countess of Villagonzalo; to Don Gregorio Toledo; and in particular to Professors Enrique Lafuente Ferrari and Ramón Stolz who have placed their expert knowledge of Goya's life, works and technique at the disposal of our readers. We would also express our gratitude to Don Dositeo Diaz Lagaron, devoted keeper of the Goya mausoleum, for his kind and helpful co-operation, and to our good friend M. Pierre Gassier who has not only made the translation of the Spanish texts for the French edition of this book but also gave much help at each stage of its preparation in coping with the many problems which inevitably arose in an enterprise of this kind.

To present in color

the cycle of frescos painted by Goya in the church of San Antonio de la Florida was an undertaking that involved considerable difficulty and we feel bound to pay homage here to our technical staff, whose resourcefulness and experienced knowledge successfully overcame the peculiar problems set by this book. The difficulty we were confronted with was that of reproducing not a succession of separate pictures but a vast mural composition, taken first in its entirety just as it appears to the naked eye in the cupola of the church fifty feet above the floor, then broken up into its component fragments and details shown in close-up. The latter were photographed by placing the camera on a scaffolding in the cupola itself, level with the frescos, and "shooting" each of the principal scenes and figure groups in continuous sequence; in this way the most striking details are brought out for the first time with vivid clarity. But great care had to be taken in order to maintain the organic harmony between the work as a whole and its different parts, and to respect the prevailing tonality of the entire fresco while at the same time bringing out in detail the intense life of forms and colors that Goya so passionately breathed into it. In this endeavor we hope to have succeeded — thanks to the skill and perseverance of our technical staff of photographers, engravers, and color printers — and thereby contributed not only to make a great masterpiece of art more widely known at present but to consecrate the greater glory it is sure to enjoy in the future.

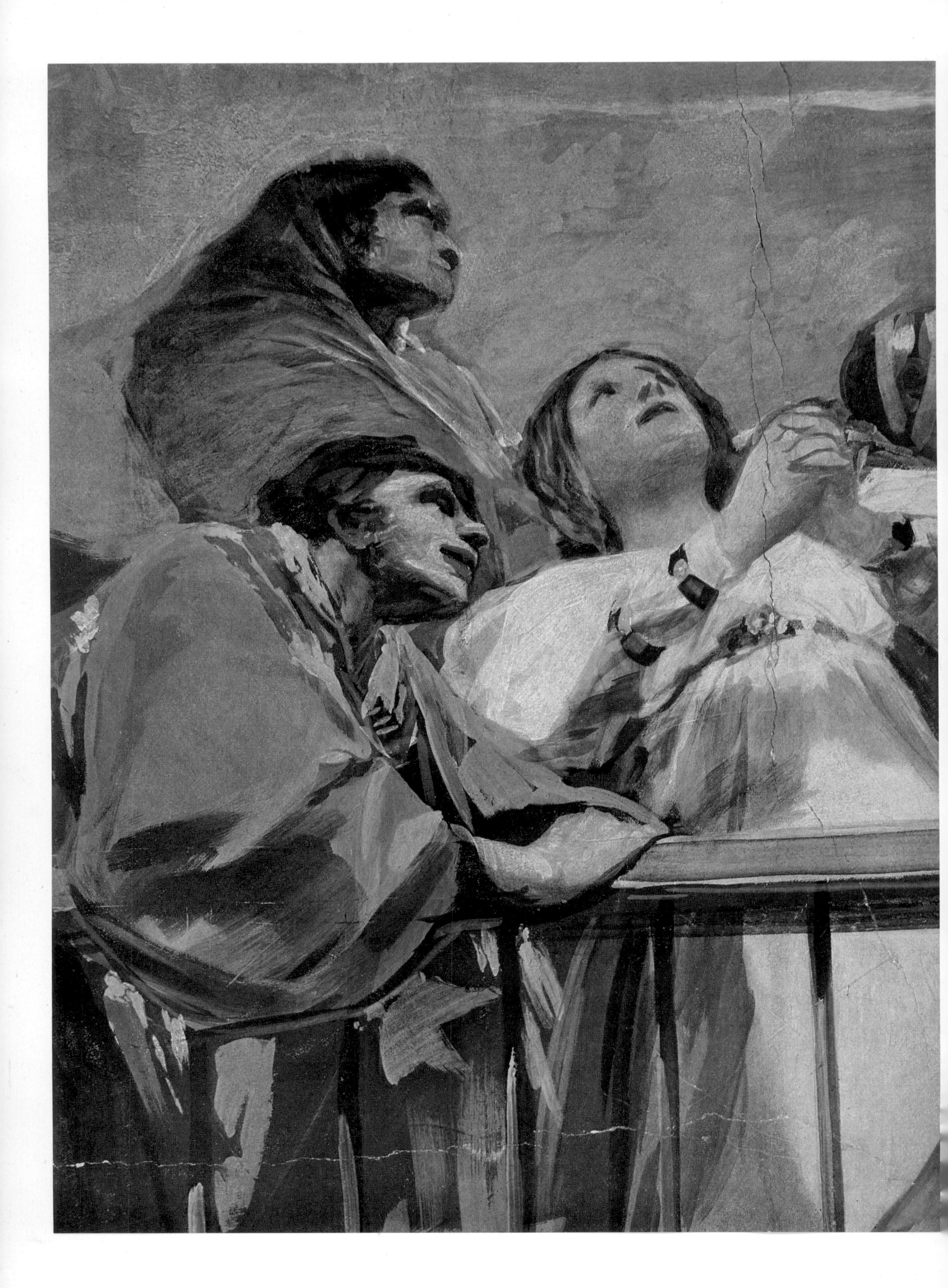

A POSTHUMOUS GENIUS

André Malraux has summed up the vicissitudes of Goya's reputation in one of those brief, pregnant phrases that are his forte: *Goya, talent célèbre, génie posthume.* Goya's contemporaries saw in him an exceptionally talented artist, a maker of admirable portraits when he was in the mood, and a man of wayward fancies who, when he turned to large-scale compositions, handled them in a highly unorthodox manner, disregarding all the art canons of the day. But his recognition as a genius was, as Malraux puts it, "posthumous"; not until our modern sensibility had been attuned, by way of Romanticism, to an appreciation of certain solitary and intriguing artists of the past, was it possible to acclaim Goya as a brilliant innovator, harbinger of a new aesthetic, born out of his due time. The publication of this book is a timely confirmation of Malraux's dictum. Today Goya ranks, by general consent, among the greatest painters the world has known; for now that, thanks to 19th-century art, our vision covers a vastly wider field than in the past, Goya's work appeals no less to the champions of an aesthetic tradition they regard as sacrosanct than to the boldest pioneers of modern art. It was his etchings that laid the foundations of Goya's cosmopolitan renown in the first instance and it was only later, when his paintings—especially his striking portraits of men and women—began to cross the frontiers of Spain, that these pictures, largely as a result of his growing fame, found their way into the great art museums of other countries.

The first quarter of the 20th century witnessed the consolidation of Goya's reputation as one of the great creators of Western painting. But even so, despite a steadily increasing interest in Goya's art, some important elements of his oeuvre have been treated as "minor" works, neglected or disparaged. Indeed we find a tendency to regard his large-scale compositions with an indifference verging on disdain, and though his dramatic evocations of war now rank among his masterpieces, his large mural decorations have been far from receiving the consideration they deserve. No full-length study of Goya's murals exists and the author of these lines has for many years been working on a project for filling this lacuna. The surviving paintings in the Carthusian monastery of Aula Dei near Saragossa have not been studied and few reproductions of them are available; nor, so far, has there been any adequate publication of the so-called Black Paintings from the "Deaf Man's House," famous though these now are. Stranger still is the fact that, in an age when color reproductions of the masterpieces of art are so much appreciated, the frescos in San Antonio de la Florida have been so rarely and scantily illustrated. Thanks to the enlightened vigilance of Albert Skira and the publication of the present volume, it is now possible for the art-loving public to become acquainted with one of the most remarkable and most broadly conceived works of the great Spanish master. Only a publication of this kind, enriched with all the attributes of color, could enable the paintings in the little church on the outskirts of Madrid to contribute to that worldwide renown which now is Goya's.

All the same it should be pointed out, in simple justice, that the frescos in San Antonio de la Florida have always been much liked in Spain, though their popularity may have owed little to their merits as works of art. The church of San Antonio is the focal point of a long-established religious festival particularly dear to the townsfolk of Madrid. On June 13, feast day of St Anthony, thousands of Madrileños have flocked since time immemorial to the banks of the Manzanares—that humble stream immortalized by its associations with Goya's art—to welcome in the spring. On these festal occasions the doors of the church containing Goya's decorations stand open and a spirit of pagan mirth combined with local piety, a traditional homage paid by life to religion and to art, reigns within the little sanctuary. True, all Spanish art critics and connoisseurs were fully alive to the peculiar charm of these frescos, unique of their kind; but until quite recently their message was lost, or almost lost, on the outside, non-Spanish world—and this chiefly for two reasons. Firstly because only the unqualified boldness of so much modern art could adjust contemporary vision to those "extreme values" which are bodied forth in Goya's art and of which the Florida cupola is assuredly one of the noblest examples. And, secondly, because the beauties of these frescos can never be apprehended by those who have not studied them *in situ*, or in faithful reproduction, as now is possible thanks to the vast technical improvements in color photography evidenced by the illustrations in this volume. By means of these the public is now enabled to appraise and admire, in all its splendor, one of Goya's most remarkable, most amazingly "modernistic" creations; paintings whose complete originality and boldness of conception were an amazing anticipation of an art undreamed-of by any of his contemporaries.

In point of fact, however, even Spanish writers on art have usually dealt with the frescos in San Antonio de la Florida rather cursorily and failed to give them their due. Looking through the pages devoted to them in almost any work on Goya, we soon see how lukewarm was the author's admiration and how he tends to sum them up in a few well-worn clichés. We are regaled with commonplaces on the "popular" aspects of Goya's art and the mundane charm of the angels—so unblushingly feminine that the Spanish novelist Doña Emilia Pardo Bazán has described them as *ángelas*—who, posted on the arches underneath the cupola and thus in full visibility, seem to be holding up heavy curtains so as to reveal the miracle taking place above. The models for these angels were, we are told, simply *majas* (gay young women of the people) or, according to another—equally far-fetched—legend, great ladies of the Court. After expounding these fantastic theories, by-products of a "Goya myth" that travesties the man that Goya really was, and after some description of the technique employed, even our most eminent art authorities seem to have felt they had said all that needed to be said. Exceptionally, a few understanding artists have appraised these pictures at their true value, but even so, they were known only by faulty, badly reproduced photographs, usually taken from below and thus giving effects of excessive foreshortening and cramping the general lay-out. Indeed it was due to a series of chance events, sometimes of a dramatic order, that an opportunity arose to see these frescos as they should be seen and study them in close-up.

The big scene in the dome represents a miracle performed by St Anthony of Padua, and it is also something of a miracle that this little church still exists. During the tragic years of the Spanish Civil War (1936-1939) Madrid was in the forefront of the battle line and for two years the church was left to take its chances in a sort of no-man's land, sometimes totally neglected and sometimes (what was worse) serving as an advanced post, a helpless witness to the savagery of war. It is miraculous indeed that San Antonio should have survived; its escape, though not unscathed, from the total destruction that then seemed inevitable may well be described as providential. No sooner was the war over than the necessary repairs were set on foot and a scaffolding was erected to enable the paintings, damaged by moisture, to be restored and the entire painted surface to be cleaned, after expert examination. Thanks to this scaffolding many Spanish and some foreign art-lovers were able for the first time to perceive the over-all significance of these pictures and the genius that had gone to their making. Those who see the frescos only from below, even with the help of field-glasses, can have no idea of the superb quality of the painting in the cupola of San Antonio. It was then that the writer, amongst others, had an opportunity for a close-up view, and the sight of the circular cortège of onlookers at the miracle performed by the saint, its rich diversity and beauty, was nothing short of a revelation to all of us. Our one regret was that (for some reason unknown to me) it was impossible to arrange for the frescos to be photographed then and there, as we all hoped would be done. We realized at once that the amazing boldness of Goya's handling of his subject outdid by far even the most daring achievements of our ultra-modern artists; that, high aloft on his scaffolding, Goya had infused the very breath of life into these strange creations of his far-ranging imagination, projected on to the concave surfaces of cupola and arches with broad, unerring brushstrokes. But he was certainly aware that, seen from below, these figures painted in a rapture of creative inspiration would give but a pale impression, a mere summary, of the vision taking form under his brush. And so things were for over a century—until, owing to the "disasters of war," a few of us were enabled to see them near at hand.

As it turned out, this seemingly unique experience was to have a sequel when Albert Skira decided to publish at least a few color plates of the San Antonio frescos. Accordingly (in April 1955) a scaffolding was set up and powerful electric lighting installed within the cupola so as to secure color photographs capable of ensuring faithful reproductions of the originals. Those of us who saw the paintings under these conditions were even more impressed than on the previous occasion. Never shall I forget the moment when, walking from Madrid to San Antonio in a warm April evening under a starry sky, I suddenly saw the windows of the little church, in which the technicians were at work, ablaze with an unwonted, preternaturally vivid light. And when, on entering, I climbed to the highest platform, level with the master's enormous, gloriously realized paintings, I felt as if I had been transported into a wonder-world of forms and colors, peopled with a motley crowd of men, women and children, interested or indifferent spectators of the miracle of the dead man recalled to life so as to reveal the name of his murderer and save an innocent man from execution.

No Renaissance painting has such an overwhelming effect on the beholder. The noble, monumental forms of classical art, essentially serene and humanist, can never produce the nervous shock we get from Goya's figures, seen thus close at hand. The original plan had been to obtain four or five color photographs to be included in a monograph on Goya's work as a whole; but after seeing the San Antonio frescos under these conditions—it was for all of us like the discovery of a new, untrodden world—Albert Skira decided for the publication of the present volume, devoted entirely to this "inimitable symphony of light and color."

SAN ANTONIO DE LA FLORIDA

THE CHURCH AND ITS HISTORY

MADRID might be described as an "abstract" capital; hitherto only an occasional residence of the Spanish kings, it was chosen by that mathematically-minded monarch Philip II (1556-1598) as the seat of government because of its situation, at the exact geographical center of his realm. Originally there was only a small town on the site and the king, it seems, appreciated this remoteness from the outside world. But in Spain nothing is ever so simple as it may seem; hence the danger of generalizations. As Eugenio d'Ors has remarked, "Madrid is a synthesis; officially a capital, actually a triumph over or, at least, an amalgam of contraries." On a hill beside the little river Manzanares there stood a medieval castle which developed into the Alcázar of the House of Austria and, in the 18th century, the palace of the Bourbon monarchy. From this vantage-point we can see the "contraries" which Madrid set out to synthesize: on one side arid wastelands, a foretaste of the dim horizons of La Mancha, land of the mirages which played havoc with Don Quixote's peace of mind; but at the foot of the palace stretches a vast panorama of the forests and sierras whose beauties Velazquez embodied in the backgrounds of his royal portraits. On the other side of the river are the Campo del Moro gardens, the Real Casa and, further on, the Pardo with its groves of evergreen oaks bounded on the horizon by the blue line of the Guadarrama. Between the palace and the river begins the Royal Road of Castile (now called the Corunna road since it ends at that famous seaport on the northwest coast). The northern railway station was built, at the end of the 19th century, on the narrow strip of land between the Montaña del Principe Pío and the left bank of the Manzanares. Beside the railway line and the station buildings, and flanking a level crossing which leads to what was called in Goya's day La Cuesta de Areneros, are two elegant neo-classical churches built on the same simple lines, with whitewashed walls and adornments and string-courses in stone. The one nearer to Madrid is the church of San Antonio de la Florida, which Goya decorated. The other, its exact replica, was built recently when it was decided to convert the original church into an art sanctuary and mausoleum.

The church (or rather "hermitage," as it has always been called) of San Antonio has a nave of modest proportions which, viewed from outside, stands out above the structures with leaded roofs that flank it and is crowned by a small, gracefully proportioned cupola ending in a lantern turret, with a pinnacle of elegantly classical design on each side.

A visitor knowing nothing of the past history of this strip of land on the bank of the Manzanares might well be puzzled by the presence of two churches on a site which, formerly the resort of picnic-parties, is now wedged in between a main road and Madrid's largest railway station. But until near the close of the 19th century "La Florida" with its woodlands and gardens was an ideal retreat for those in quest of solitude and silence. The hermitage was outside the city near the Puerta de San Vicente, one of the old gates of Madrid, which stood where there is now the plaza fronting the northern railway terminus.

At the city gates (no longer in existence) were stationed representatives of the royal treasury whose duty it was to inspect all goods entering the town, levy the appropriate toll dues and check as best they could the activities of the smugglers who plied a thriving trade in Goya's time. One of his tapestry cartoons shows armed guards of the Tobacco Service keeping watch on the foreshore of the Manzanares, with the Sierra in the background [1].

In those days of fervent piety these excisemen were provided with places of worship for their special use and beside several city gates was a hermitage dedicated to a patron saint. One such stood near the Puerta de San Vicente; originally dedicated to the Virgin of Grace, it had long been known as the hermitage of St Anthony owing to the fact that a statue of that saint had been installed in it. In Goya's time, when mention was made of "the saint," either San Isidro (patron of Madrid) or San Antonio de la Florida was always meant. This hermitage, it seems, had been in existence since the 16th century. Originally it was a very humble shrine, containing merely an image in a little shelter, set up for the use of the women who came down daily to this stretch of the river bank to do their washing; they, too, figure in one of Goya's tapestry cartoons [2]. A second chapel was promoted to the rank of church in the course of the 18th century, when the Guarda Mayor, Don Francisco del Olmo, commissioned the Baroque architect Churriguera to build a new church in brick. It was completed in 1732. There a new effigy of St Anthony, made by the sculptor Juan de Villanueva (father of the famous neo-classical architect), was installed; ever since then the church has borne the name of the Franciscan saint, and San Antonio de la Florida been one of the most frequented sanctuaries of the district [3].

The royal domain (the Alcázar Park, commonly styled Campo del Moro) ended near the San Vicente gate. La Florida and the land around it were private property, consisting of country houses and gardens owned by the nobility of Madrid and religious communities such as that of San Jerónimo which, during the reign of Henry IV (1453-1474), established itself in the El Paso Monastery. Just beyond the railway station is a hill known as La Montaña del Principe Pío because it once was owned by a member of the Pío family of Savoy, the Marquis of Castel-Rodrigo. Amongst the original owners of estates in this district were the Count of Noblejas, the Count of La Moncloa [4] and the Duchess of Alba, Goya's patroness. Teixera's plan of Madrid [5], dated 1656, gives a good idea of the topography of this region and, though the map was made over a hundred years before Goya started work on his frescos, it would seem that few changes had taken place prior to the building of the now-existing church of San Antonio.

It was Charles III, king of Spain in the Age of Enlightenment and Reform, who elevated Madrid to the rank of a great capital. Under his auspices handsome public buildings were erected in all parts of the country and La Florida was not neglected. The track leading from La Cuesta de San Vicente to the river bank was converted into a carriageable road; in order to enlarge it and provide for spacious verges, it was necessary to demolish the church of San Antonio built by Churriguera and by now affiliated to the Benedictine Abbey of San Martín at Madrid. In 1766 Mass was solemnized in San Antonio for the last time before it was pulled down. Charles III gave orders for its rebuilding near by and Francesco Sabatini, an eminent Italian architect much in favor at the court, drew up the plans. To this master of classical architecture Madrid owes several fine buildings, amongst them the Real Aduana (now Ministry of Finance) and the Puerta de Alcalá. The Puerta de San Vicente, which no longer exists, was also built to his plans in 1775, at the same time as the new church.

This San Vicente gate had but a brief existence. Soon after it was built Charles IV (who came to the throne in 1788) decided to add fresh lands to his domain by including more of the picturesque country skirting the Manzanares and expropriating local landowners. Now that the "royal road" had been opened up, the La Florida woodlands had become a favorite resort and the drive to San Vicente a fashionable excursion. Moreover the Duchess of Alba's palace had attracted to the district the high society of Madrid, and this contributed no doubt to drawing the Court's attention to the amenities of La Florida. Charles IV—or rather his impulsive wife Maria Luisa—decided to have a secluded country place on the left bank of the Manzanares and after the queen had followed, so to speak, in the footsteps of the duchess, her favorite Godoy, then at the height of his ascendancy, bought (in 1795) the La Moncloa gardens which had come on to the market after the suppression of the Jesuit order.

In 1792 Charles IV had given instructions for the acquisition of the palace and so-called "La Florida gardens"—that is to say, the estate of the Marquis of Castel-Rodrigo (La Montaña del Principe Pío) and the majorat of Romanillos. In the following years he bought several neighboring properties so as to round off the royal demesne [6].

Thus La Florida developed into a handsome estate owned by the Crown and so remained until 1866, when Queen Isabella II ceded it to the State. The Northern Railway was then under construction and the line was to pass, parallel to the "royal road," through La Florida up to the Manzanares bridge. Accordingly, a strip of land beside the Montaña del Principe Pío was made over to the railway company, for the station; unfortunately no one could then foresee the drawbacks of this site, which allowed no possibility of enlarging the station yards to cope with the increased traffic of later years. The transfer of this land to the railway and its after-effects provoked violent press campaigns, and in 1871 the Government instituted legal proceedings against the Northern Railway Company, proceedings which, after dragging on interminably, led (so far as I can ascertain) to no result [7].

The alterations made in La Florida necessitated the immediate demolition of the church of San Antonio. In the year when the purchases of adjoining estates began (that is to say in 1792) the King issued orders for the acquisition from the Hieronymite Order, who had established themselves opposite the Abanico fountain, of "all the land needful for erecting on this site the new chapel of San Antonio" after the demolition of the former chapel [8].

In the records of the Royal Palace are entries clearing up a point hitherto in doubt: the name of the architect commissioned to make the new church. This was Don Felipe Fontana (not "Francisco" as used sometimes to be said, owing to a misunderstanding easily accounted for, which will be discussed below). Who was this Fontana? There is little documentary evidence available regarding this Italian architect who worked at Madrid in the reign of Charles IV and his personality remains something of a mystery.

A small pamphlet relating to the building of the new church helped to perpetuate the error referred to above. The few persons under whose eyes it came—amongst them Don Elías Tormo, my teacher [9]—took the statements of its anonymous author at their face value. This matter will be dealt with presently; for the time being I shall merely summarize such information as can be gleaned from the archives of the Royal Palace, which, though sadly incomplete, have something to say about the little known architect responsible for San Antonio.

Among the memoranda submitted to the king during the decade in which the church was built is one in which Fontana describes himself as "architect, painter and stage-setter at the theater of El Buen Retiro." It is a matter of record that the king appointed him to this post on May 13, 1790 [10]. Presumably he was one of the Italian architects who were working under the supervision of Sabatini. In his petitions he alludes to the "numerous" works he carried out in his capacity of painter and architect; actually, however, San Antonio is the only one that can so far be positively ascribed to him. The records of the Royal Palace inform us that work began on April 22, 1792, and in his memorandum Fontana declares that the church "is built after his plans and under his supervision, in his capacity of architect specially appointed for this purpose by His Majesty"—which removes any possible doubt as to the identity of the builder of this church [11].

King Charles IV was present at the laying of the foundation stone[12] and, following a long-established custom, coins bearing the reigning monarch's effigy were buried beneath it. The site selected lay "between the old and new Areneros roads," and work continued until 1798, when the church was ready to be opened for worship, if we are to trust the curious pamphlet referred to above. It is entitled *Notícia del motivo o causa de la fundación y dedicación de la capilla de San Antonio de Padua llamada de la Florida y mudanzas que ha habido en ella hasta el presente año desde su primera fundación...* The text of this brochure is something of a miscellany, comprising as well as the history of the church a recapitulation of Father Croisset's Life of St Anthony, a eulogy in verse of the new statue of the saint and the newly built church, and concluding with an envoy addressed to King Charles. Though of little literary merit, the first of the two poems is of interest since it confirms the attribution of the church to Fontana, already mentioned in the prose section of the pamphlet (with the erroneous version of his first name given above) [13].

The ceremonial inauguration of the church took place on July 11, 1799, almost a year after Goya had finished his frescos [14]. Perhaps the king did not wish to open it for public worship until the question of his ecclesiastical autonomy had been settled once for all. The special interest felt by the king and queen in their La Florida demesne is evidenced by the fact that they went to the pains of obtaining from Pope Pius VI a papal brief, dated July 30, 1798, in virtue of which La Florida was no longer included in the parish of San Martín's Abbey and was brought under the control of the Chapel Palatine which, by a brief of June 23, 1753, Pope Benedict XIV had raised to the rank of an independent parish under the administration of the First Chaplain of the Army, the Patriarch of the Indies and the priest attached to the Royal Court. Actually the sole effect of the brief of 1798 was to enlarge the authority of the Chapel Palatine in such a way that La Florida and the Church of San Antonio could benefit by the privileged position it now enjoyed.

There is a copy of the brief in the archives of the Royal Palace, Madrid; it enumerates the estates which, after being incorporated in La Florida, became church property. The copy is authenticated by Don Leandro Fernández de Moratín, a contemporary writer and a friend of Goya; at the time (1798) he was a member of His Majesty's Privy Council in the capacity of secretary and member of the Bureau of Translation. To give an idea of the vast extent of the royal domain of La Florida we need only mention that in the 19th century it still had no less than forty gates, six in ironwork. The one nearest the church was called the Gate of San Antonio.

THE BIOGRAPHICAL CONTEXT

Although the extant records, as we have seen, have much to tell us about the building of the church, the same cannot be said of the paintings within it. Even before the publication of any document bearing on them, however, their ascription to Goya had never been questioned, in view of the trustworthy witness accounts that had come down from well-informed contemporaries such as Goya's son Xavier. In the biographical sketch of his father which he gave Carderera, and which was found among the latter's papers, we read: "He painted frescos at Saragossa and in San Antonio de la Florida" [15]. Carderera, himself a painter, was personally acquainted with Goya and at one time hoped to study under him. This was at Madrid in 1816, when his patron Palafox, a friend of Goya, commended him to the master [16].

Strangely enough, however, among the many records concerning Goya in the archives of the Royal Palace [17], the only one relating to the San Antonio frescos that has been found is a brief statement of account for materials supplied to the artist "for the work in the chapel of San Antonio de la Florida, which he carried out at His Majesty's bidding in this year, 1798." It is dated December 20, 1798, and was first published by the Count of La Viñaza in 1887. Since then it has been published and commented on many times [18].

Some account of Goya's career up to the time he painted the San Antonio frescos seems called for at this point. Most important of all to remember is the severe illness of 1792, which struck him down at the age of forty-six, at the height of his powers, and left an indelible mark both on his life and on his art. Before that he had worked hard and nourished high ambitions. He had undertaken tasks whose futility must have been obvious to him and performed them conscientiously. He had made his way, slowly and doggedly, along the beaten track leading to royal favor and had endured, if with ill-disguised reluctance, the domination of his brother-in-law Francisco Bayeu, whose frigidity and pedantry were diametrically opposed to his own temperament. His efforts had been rewarded. In 1780 he was elected a member of the Academy of San Fernando; in 1783 he painted the portrait of the Infante Don Luis, the king's brother, who had become his patron; this was followed by the portrait of Count Floridablanca, chief minister of state to Charles III. In a few years' time Goya had established himself as the favorite portrait-painter of the Spanish aristocracy; he moved in Court circles and stood on friendly terms with the most enlightened men of the day. When Charles IV came to the throne in 1788, he was kept busy producing portraits of the new king and queen, and early in 1789 was appointed Court Painter. But these were troubled times. Hardly had the reign of Charles IV begun when the French Revolution broke out, rousing the apprehensions of all the monarchs of Europe and the hopes of all liberals, and amongst the latter were Goya's closest friends. But despite the storm-clouds gathering on the political horizon, Goya now entered upon a period of great prosperity and immense productiveness. Then in 1792, without warning, he fell victim to a terrible disease that, when at last his life was out of danger, left him stone deaf and threatened for a time to put an end to his career as a painter [19].

Medical men are still at variance as to the true nature of that disease. Some have diagnosed syphilis, but Goya's friend Jovellanos described it as "apoplexy." In any event, it led to a clean-cut break in his life which is reflected in his work. His deafness cut him off from society, but, as we can now see, this was far from being detrimental to his art. Nor did "the crises of Goya's life," as Gómez Moreno calls them, ever produce changes of style drastic enough to interrupt the evolution of his genius. The body of work produced by Goya in the course of his long career has in fact much greater continuity than many art critics would have us believe. What happened is simply that, with the passing years and the buffets of fate, the qualities peculiar to Goya's personal aesthetic were intensified; indeed misfortune acted as a stimulus. He says as much in that often-quoted letter he addressed to Don Bernardo Iriarte in 1794, when, speaking of the pictures he then was working on, he claimed to have succeeded in recording "impressions that have no place in works made to order, in which so little scope is left for fantasy and originality."

The 1792 attack drove him in upon himself and by the same token deepened his pessimistic outlook on the world at large, his scorn of social conventions, his sarcastic turn of mind and, last but not least, his imagination. All this was soon to be reflected in his art. During the enforced inertia and isolation of his convalescence, his mind was full of half-fledged ideas, obsessive forms, new visions of reality, and little by little, day by day, the seemingly incoherent elements of his day-dreams fell into a pattern. Evoked by sickness and his seclusion from society, there arose from the depths of his subconscious self a horde of phantom figures, strange creations of his fevered fancy, and these he made haste to record with all the artistic means at his disposal. Matured in solitude, his disdain of orthodox art and all set rules grew stronger and more than ever he felt the need to express himself with uncompromising sincerity, in a language of forms and colors destined to inaugurate a new art era. He found release, the catharsis he was looking for, in a novel, personal, wholly original idiom, the perfect medium for expressing both the weird inventions of his fancy and his profound disillusionment. The result was *The Caprices.* Always exceptionally active, his visual imagination acquired a feverish intensity now that deafness had surrounded him with walls of silence. Keenly observant of movements, features and attitudes, he accumulated in his memory a mass of data which he faithfully recorded in a kind of pictorial shorthand. To this hypersensitiveness of the eye was added the temperamental violence and irritability of a man of indomitable energy, laid low by a sudden illness, handicapped by deafness, and embittered by a stroke of unbelievable bad luck at the very time when his artistic powers had reached their zenith. *The Caprices* express all this; they embody the spleen of Goya's reaction to his malady and his grievances against a world from which he was now excluded.

With the clarity which isolation gives he flayed the failings of his contemporaries. The Court circle of well-bred men and women, whose applause he had so much relished before his health collapsed, seemed to him now a sink of iniquity, a grotesque resort of ignorance, vanity, sloth and injustice. To expose these evil practices in all their naked ugliness he tortured forms and cruelly distorted them so as to wrest from them their shameful secrets. He turned a pitiless eye on his fellow men and unmasked their stupidity, the void within. For he saw the corruption and shams of social intercourse both at the Court and among the people, and despised the frivolous pleasures in which he could no longer share. In these etchings, in which he kept back nothing, Goya obviously voiced, if with a wholly personal outspokenness, the critical attitude of his enlightened Spanish friends towards the social order of the day. *The Caprices,* then, are more than a bold flight into the fantastic, spiced with personal allusions; they are a fierce indictment of the entire social system, of all institutions and persons in authority—doubly potent for being a consummate work of art.

If I dwell on *The Caprices* at some length, this is because, in some respects, they point the way to that expressionist distortion of the human figure which is one of the most striking innovations of the San Antonio frescos. Without quite bringing it into the open, *The Caprices* give the first clear signs of that procedure typical of Goya's handling of form, which might be described as *the distorting variation* and which from now on was to be so distinctive a feature of his art.

During his convalescence Goya worked hard at *The Caprices* and on paintings in which he could give free rein to his imagination; he gave no thought to his former patrons but worked almost exclusively for his own satisfaction. By the time he had fully recovered and returned to normal life, he was already well on the way to achieving the complete liberty of expression he had always aspired to. Some of the portraits of this period attain a rare perfection: that of his brother-in-law *Francisco Bayeu* in grey (Prado), that of the *Duchess of Alba* in a black mantilla (Hispanic Society, New York), and—of particular interest here—that of the actress *La Tirana* (Academy of San Fernando, Madrid), which has so much in common with the figure-paintings at San Antonio de la Florida.

Spanish political life, too, had entered upon a period of convulsive change. The all-powerful Godoy, the queen's favorite, now suffered his first diplomatic setback. The desultory war with France ended in the treaty of Basel (1795), by the terms of which Bourbon Spain was forced into incongruous alliance with the French Republic. And in 1797 the changed political situation brought two friends of Goya to the fore: Saavedra, appointed minister of finance, and Jovellanos, minister of justice.

For years illness and convalescence had slowed Goya's output down to a mere trickle, but now he made up for lost time. With his friends in power he was in a position to solicit favors and obtain them. On March 22, 1798, he presented a petition asking for payment of the arrears "that were due to him." "Six years ago," he explained, "my health broke down completely. My hearing in particular has suffered, and I have grown so deaf that without the sign-language of the hands I cannot understand what people are saying. It was therefore impossible for me to practise my profession during this period." He expressed the hope that he would continue to receive a salary for his assistant, who ground his colors and whom he could not dispense with, since, as he wrote, "his help is absolutely necessary if I am to carry out the work Your Majesty may deign to entrust me with." This petition proves that as late as March 1798 Goya had not yet been commissioned to paint the San Antonio frescos; had it been otherwise, he would have mentioned the fact to justify the need of an assistant. With his friends in power and no doubt aware that a large fresco commission was in the offing, Goya's petition was transmitted to the king at once and favorably received. Even in the past Jovellanos had shown his willingness to supply Goya with orders. In 1784 he had commissioned him to do some altar-paintings (now lost) for the church of Calatrava College at Salamanca; in 1796 he tried to obtain an order for Goya to do the portrait of the Prince of Asturias, who then seemed likely to assume the leadership of a party hostile to Godoy; in 1798, at Aranjuez, Goya made a portrait of Jovellanos, who had just been appointed minister, and shortly after one of Saavedra. This justifies us in assuming that, since he was in a position of authority at the time, it was Jovellanos who obtained the San Antonio de la Florida commission for Goya, thus helping the artist financially in a time of need.

Though they were honest and responsible ministers, capable perhaps of radically amending the policy of Charles IV and repairing the blunders of Godoy, Goya's friends remained in power for only a short time. In August 1798, when Goya was on the point of beginning the San Antonio frescos, Jovellanos resigned; Saavedra followed suit in 1799. Godoy was reinstated and adopted a foolhardy foreign policy leading to the collapse of Spanish sea power at Trafalgar (1805) and the Napoleonic invasion of Spain (1808).

THE INTERIOR OF THE CHURCH

San Antonio is built in the form of a Greek cross, with the addition of a basket-handle shaped apse. The extreme shortness of the arms of the cross emphasizes the spaciousness of the rectangular crossing above which rises a cupola resting on pendentives, with a lantern turret at the summit. The width of the nave, roughly equal to that of a side of the central crossing, is nineteen feet; this gives an idea of the dimensions of the cupola Goya was called on to decorate. The foot of the cross has the same width, and measures eleven feet in length, while its top measures thirteen and a half feet, and the apse proper about ten feet in its central part. The church is elegantly designed, its proportions could hardly be bettered, and we can see that Fontana had studied to good effect the canons of the best classical architecture. Except in the projecting pilasters and the moldings on the pediment, we find nothing of the exuberance of Italian Baroque, which, thanks to the foreign architects imported by the Bourbons, had become acclimatized in Madrid.

Three steps with rounded edges lead up to the harmoniously planned front portal, crowned by an arched pediment, above which is the window, surmounted by a deep, molded cornice, which lights the near end of the church. The external pilasters are quite plain, as is the pediment; the only ornament on the façade was a handsome escutcheon displaying the arms of Spain with the royal crown and Golden Fleece. This was destroyed during the 1868 revolution, but can be seen in early photographs [20]. The interior is simple to the point of austerity, despite the use of Corinthian capitals. Plain pilasters with daintily patterned capitals tell out against simulated pilasters, adding a note of grace and delicacy to the small, bijou-like interior. The architect has shown much skill in his highly restrained treatment of the entablature: an architrave in three staggered bands, a quite plain frieze, a finely carved cornice underpinned by modillions. Such elements as stand out, owing to the general disposition of the edifice, are particularly noticeable in the transept crossing, where the elegant purity of Fontana's style can be seen at its best. The choir is divided from the transept by a row of steps; leaning against the front of the marble high altar, which stands between two pilasters in the recess formed by the concave wall, are two kneeling angels who seem on the point of taking wing. Stucco figures in the purest classical Italian style, they differ *toto caelo* from the delightfully feminine creations of Goya's brush. These angels are adoring the symbol of the Trinity, a triangle wreathed in golden rays; one of them with his hands clasped, the other pressing them to his breast. And somehow, very different though they are, the angels painted by Goya in the hemisphere of the apse seem to be joining in this act of adoration.

The side-altars are in red and green marble and decorated with naked cherubs. The choice of the pictures adorning these altars was ill-advised, to say the least of it; productions of the King's Painter, Jacinto Gómez Pastor, and sadly uninspired, they were not worthy of being sheltered under the same roof as Goya's brilliant creations. The picture on the right-hand altar depicts St Louis of France and San Isidro Labrador; on the left is an Immaculate Conception (the youthful Virgin is quite lamentable) with St Ferdinand and San Carlo Borromeo paying homage. In the walls of each of the arms of the crossing preceding the choir is a door with elegant moldings and an arched pediment. The locks have inscriptions recording the date when the two doors were made: *Año de 1796*. That on the left leads to the old sacristy; in its vestibule we can see the niche which contained the font for ritual ablutions; it is in white marble, with an arch above, and bears the inscription: *Año de 1798*.

Flanking the walls, in the arms of the cross, are big arches whose intrados were painted by Goya, the painted areas being sunk slightly below the level of two smooth, undecorated bands framing them on either side. Below the arches and above the cornice are the transept windows by which the nave is lighted; the wall surfaces alongside the windows also have paintings by Goya. In all he painted fourteen portions of the church: four intrados, four strips of wall flanking the side-windows, the cupola, the apse and four pendentives.

In the median line of the church, on the steps leading up to the choir, a slanting block of granite marks the artist's tomb; its only decoration is a cross and an inscription in bronze letters: *GOYA, Nació en Fuendetodos el 31 de marzo de 1746. Murió en Burdeos el 16 de abril de 1828* (born at Fuendetodos, March 31, 1746; died at Bordeaux, April 16, 1828). Embedded in the center of the granite block is the convex limestone monument which had stood on his grave in the cemetery of Bordeaux; on it is engraved the following inscription [21]:

HIC JACET
FRANCISCUS A GOYA ET LUCIENTES
HISPANIENSIS PERITISSIMUS PICTOR
MAGNAQUE SUI NOMINIS
CELEBRITATE NOTUS
DECURSO PROBE LUMINE VITAE
OBIIT XVI KALENDAS MAII
ANNO DOMINI
M.DCCC.XXVIII
AETATIS SUAE
LXXXV
R. I. P.

THE FRESCOS IN THE CUPOLA

HERE and in the following pages will be found an historical and factual description of Goya's frescos, beginning with the Miracle of St Anthony, depicted in the cupola. In this, the central scene, Goya was called on to illustrate the miraculous resurrection of a murdered man, summoned up from the grave to testify to the innocence of Don Martín Bulloes, a Portuguese gentleman of good family and the saint's father, who was accused of murder. The tale was of the type that had been popularized by the Golden Legend and, as on previous occasions of this sort [22], Goya utilized the iconographic sources most familiar to the public—in this case Father Croisset's *Christian Year* which, in the Spanish version by Father José Francisco Isla, was then being widely read in Spain. This is how the miracle is described in the text used by Goya. "He (St Anthony) was in Padua when he got news that his father was about to be condemned to death on a false charge of murder. He asked leave of his Father Superior to proceed to Portugal and in a flash was miraculously transported to Lisbon. There he confronted the judges and solemnly averred his father's innocence and, having failed to convince them, asked that the corpse of the victim should be brought to the courtroom. Then he questioned the dead man, bidding him in the name of Our Lord Jesus Christ to say in a loud voice, understandable by all, if his father was the man responsible for his death. Whereupon the corpse arose and publicly declared that the accused man was innocent; after which declaration he sank back again into his bier. Well indeed may we understand the amazement and the awe of all the beholders."

Goya keeps to the main lines of the narrative as given in the *Christian Year*, but treats the incident in a forthright, free and highly personal manner. For one thing he refrains, and very rightly, from depicting an interior scene (the courtroom), as he would have had to do had he kept strictly to Father Croisset's text. Similarly he rejects all the time-honored devices of the earlier painters of cupolas: clouds, soaring angels, visions of opened heavens, circling cherubim. Also he rules out all effects of perspective. In short he does away with those spectacular procedures which bulked so large in the works of the Renaissance painters handling such subjects (for example Correggio) and were taken over and stepped up to their maximum intensity in the Baroque epoch by such artists as Guercino, Pietro da Cortona, Pozzo, Baciccio, Luca Giordano and fresco-painters of the Germanic school. Rejecting all the artifices by which these earlier cupola-painters had simplified their task, Goya went straight to the heart of the matter. The first thing was clearly to demarcate the circular space to be covered within the cupola, but without employing, as Correggio had done in Parma Cathedral, a simulated wooden ledge, a sort of wainscoting on which persons were seated, with their legs dangling above the heads of the beholder—a solution giving the artist scope for those *di sotto in sù* illusionist effects of which the Italian painter was a past-master. Nor did Goya employ one of those handsome balustrades in white marble which so often figure in the work of the Venetians, from Veronese to Tiepolo.

All Goya shows us is a plain wooden railing, like those used in his day for balconies and staircases. The spectators of the miracle are leaning on it like the crowd in a grandstand watching an open-air performance—a lay-out sometimes employed by the Venetians in their depictions of public festivals or heaven-scaling apotheoses. (Tiepolo made use of it in the Palazzo Labia at Venice and in the Villa Cordellina at Montecchio.) Actually, however, Goya's railing has less resemblance to that in front of a grandstand at some public spectacle than to the circular fence running round a Spanish bull-ring and we are shown a small boy astride it *à la toreador*; also, at one point a big sheet is hung over it, like the shawls hung over balconies at fiestas.

Beruete, speaking of San Antonio, alludes to the superb decorations of Mantegna in the Bridal Chamber of the Ducal Palace at Mantua: that fine flower of the purest Renaissance style, serene, without a hint of cheap rhetorical effect, which once seen is unforgettable. There, too, we have a balustrade rendered in true perspective with playful cherubs peeping over it or precariously perched upon the cornice. Also, like Goya's seraphs, they have tiny butterfly-wings. But the resemblance is vague at best and in any case the ideas behind these decorations, like the temperaments of the two artists, Goya and Mantegna, are poles apart. While it is clear that Goya decided not to follow in the footsteps of his immediate predecessors, the Baroque painters, it seems no less unlikely that he would have taken a lead from Mantegna and his eminently sedate, well-tempered art, with its fine purity and austerity of line.

There would be more justification for citing in this context the apse painted by Guido Reni in St Andrew's Chapel in the Church of San Gregorio Magno in Rome where we also have clothed and naked seraphs with butterfly-wings. This, as it so happens, is one of Guido's serenest works and, in its case, Mantegna's influence might reasonably be inferred. But none of this has any bearing on Goya's achievement in San Antonio de la Florida.

Nor are there any reminiscences of architecture, such as we so often find in the work of Baroque painters, even those of Spanish origin, for example Claudio Coello. In these frescos Goya had recourse to color only, color that, flooded with light, could build up forms without the need of line. Thus he created what he described as *la magia del ambiente* and "the magic of the ambiance" [23] was what he aimed at above all in his free, rapidly executed paintings in the cupola. The circular wooden barrier and stepped tiers in the background remind one of the seating arrangements in an arena when a corrida is in progress; indeed the way in which Goya presents some of the figures, crowding them up against the railing, anticipates some of the etchings he made many years later for the *Tauromachia* sequence.

The San Antonio paintings have given rise to highly conflicting opinions; many critics have tended to belittle those in the cupola and focused their interest—and their eulogies—almost exclusively on the winged figures of the angels. Don Pedro de Madrazo, who always adopted a cautious, ironical tone when dealing with Goya, wrote as follows in 1880, in a biography of the artist published in *Almanaque del Ilustración Española y Americana*: "In the church of San Antonio de la Florida on the bank of the Manzanares he painted the cupola and other frescos subsidiary to it; the miracle performed by the saint is treated as light-heartedly as if it were the performance of a troupe of strolling acrobats, while the androgynous angels have the flashing eyes and camellia-hued skin which would better become the beauty of a harlot than that of a celestial being."

Though fully alive to the high artistic merits of the paintings in the cupola, Ceferino Araujo in his study of Goya (Madrid, 1896) stresses the "unabashed realism" of the scene. "Goya has simply reproduced the groups of Spanish ladies, *majas*, children and townsfolk whom he encountered daily in the Madrid streets, upon a background that is obviously the Guadarrama range of mountains." As against this, it might be pointed out that though there are figures whose costumes may very well be those of Goya's contemporaries, we find others whose rich apparel strikes an exotic, almost biblical note, and some who wear what might be described as "Russian smocks"—garments which Goya could not possibly

UTH).

first fragment

have seen in the streets of Madrid. In any case, what above all interests us today in the work we are discussing is not at all its point of departure—i.e. the iconography, influences and intentions behind it—but the work of art in its final state, the transposition into form and color of the artist's initial vision and the way this was accomplished. For inevitably the program in the artist's mind before he takes up his brush is made to undergo in the course of realization what, following Malraux, we would call a metamorphosis.

In his *Goya, composiciones y figuras* (Madrid, 1917) Beruete rightly points out that Goya was entirely uninfluenced by any previous work of the same nature or any art tradition; that in fact "these compositions have no direct forerunners—a phenomenon all but unique in art." But he contradicts himself when in the same breath he asserts that "this is a religious scene handled by an artist in the naturalistic manner in vogue at the close of the 18th century, an artist who was eminently a man of his time, if gifted with supreme originality and far-ranging genius; that is all that need be said, but it suffices." This is at best a half-truth. For these paintings have nothing in common with those we would expect of a naturalistic painter, one that is to say who makes but little use of his imagination. Nor have Goya's frescos any of the characteristics of the art that prevailed all over Europe in the 18th century, as is clear when we compare them with the work of other painters of the period.

A. L. Mayer (in *Francisco de Goya*, Madrid, 1925) tells us that in these paintings Goya expressed himself "in a manner at once popular and modish" and believes that he was influenced by Correggio's frescos in Parma Cathedral.

In his monograph *Las pinturas del panteón de Goya, San Antonio de la Florida* (Barcelona, 1944), illustrated with photographs taken by himself, Hans Rothe expresses much the same view. "What Goya has painted is not a scene of a religious order but a sort of popular fiesta." True, it is quite obvious that Goya embodied reminiscences of popular festivals he had seen; but he transfigured these by his handling of light, by the introduction of curious figures conjured up by his imagination and by the intense vibrancy he imparted to the entire picture surface—a far cry from any actual visual experience of such scenes, which at most gave him his starting-off point. Nevertheless an understanding critic of Goya, Juan de la Encina, shows no great admiration of the San Antonio paintings; least of all of those in the cupola, which he regards as the "feeblest part" of the ensemble[24].

"The magic of the ambiance," this is what Goya sought to render in the cupola; he had no wish to illustrate an incident, to produce pious art for the gratification of true believers of a sentimental turn of mind or to commemorate an ancient legend cherished by the populace of Madrid. The unity to which he aspired was not merely one of a linear order, envisaged from the descriptive point of view and linking the figures each to each; nor yet that of an emotional communion, unambiguous and unbroken, between the various personages, a communion in which we would be invited to participate not only with our eyes but in our hearts. It is the unity of execution, of technique, that makes the entire fresco throb with a uniform vibration throughout, despite abrupt, well-nigh savage brushstrokes, despite splashes of color bold to the point of crudeness and distortions verging on sheer caricature. These are what create that atmosphere of feverish animation which reigns in the cupola, and that strongly emotive polyphony of forms and colors in which certain notes, taken by themselves, mean nothing, but in combination build up a fugue woven in threads of independent melody and rich in tempestuous sonorities scored for full orchestra by a master hand.

THE MIRACLE SCENE

AND ITS FIGURES

LEANING on the balustrade or standing behind it, the figures are spaced out on several adjacent planes, and perhaps what strikes one most at first sight in this scene is the great diversity of human types included in it: people of all ages, members of all social strata and stemming, judging by their facial structure, from widely differing racial origins. Where did Goya get his ideas for this motley assortment of humanity? No doubt some of his models were people he could have seen in contemporary Madrid: for instance the women with high-waisted dresses and white mantillas. Goya was never much concerned with accurately rendering "period" costumes, though so as to lend a touch of local color to his historical compositions he often included a figure wearing the Spanish 17th-century ruff; this sort of pictorial cliché was the furthest he ever went in reconstructions of the past. But we should be hard put to it to assign an origin to the figures in the "Miracle": for example those men bearded like apostles or those queer creatures all skin-and-bone and clad in garments impossible to date, with distraught eyes, who seem to have stepped out of a Dostoevsky novel. Then there are elegant young women, other women of a more dubious category, old men with flowing beards, some with the brooding air of ancient sages, sturdy young fellows obviously very full of themselves, peasants, children, bawds and beggars, wraithlike starvelings and nondescripts, their features briefly indicated with slashing brushstrokes making their faces seem ravaged by some ugly skin-disease. No less than fifty persons are massed around the cupola, which is barely nineteen feet in diameter.

Obviously there was a serious danger that the over-all unity of the scene might be impaired by the presence of so many people, representing such very different types of humanity and deriving from the most varied periods and milieux; some of them playing an active part in what is taking place, others merely looking on; some stricken with awe and wonder, and others seemingly indifferent, totally unmoved. Here, what holds the composition together is not any unity of action, time or place, but a unity of a technical, purely pictorial order, and the unifying principle is rhythm, a uniform vibration of the picture surface, an all-pervading textural excitement produced by juxtaposed touches, broad streaks of color, and visible traces of each brushstroke. As in many of Goya's pictures, the impression of a fully integrated whole is created by the movement paths of the composition; even the isolated, self-centered onlookers, not participating, so far as one can judge, in any collective crowd emotion, present what might be called a counterpoint of attitudes that implements the over-all effect.

We are given only the vaguest idea of the place which is the scene of the miracle. In the southwest sector [25] rises a tall curved tree whose grey-green leafage touches the base of the lantern overhead; a little to the west are other trees whose forms are blurred, and clumps of shrubs on softly modulated tones of green. More to the right we faintly see the outlines of a mountain range with specks of white near the summits, and above them a big patch of indigo sky. In the rest of the scene the sky is covered with lowering clouds, all in flat strips with rounded edges, like horizontal friezes in a stage-set.

The church of San Antonio de la Florida faces north. On entering by the main portal (now usually kept locked; one is admitted by a small side door) the visitor has the scene of the miracle immediately in front of him, since it occupies the northern hemisphere of the cupola, immediately above the beginning of the choir. Here we give a photograph of the cupola turned the way in which one sees it on entering the church. Numbers refer the reader to the descriptions of the central miracle scene and the adjoining figure groups.

1 Against the background of grey clouds shines out the yellowish halo of the saint, who is standing on an eminence. He is bending forward, gazing intently at the man whom he has called back to transitory life and whom he seems to be addressing, making the Greek gesture of benediction and bidding him declare the truth about his death. At his feet the resuscitated man, sitting on a stool and supported by one of the bystanders who has clasped his arms around his waist, is looking up at the saint with an air of meek submission. The saint might be any young monk; there is little spirituality in the face[26]. The body of the man restored to life shows how effective was Goya's technique of small, scattered brushstrokes for giving the idea of volume. Line is submerged by color, yet the plastic values of the head are rendered with complete precision.

The individuality of each of the eight figures composing the group facing the saint is so marked that it is possible to build up a sort of legend round each, arbitrary no doubt, but helpful for purposes of identification. Thus Rothe names the man who is holding up the resuscitated corpse "the man with the doglike gaze," such is the humble, doglike devotion expressed by the white-rimmed eyes. A woman, perhaps the saint's mother, is standing with her arms extended and gazing up at him with an expression of mingled grief and awe; this figure, done in ochre with touches of blue, is less clearly defined than those of the two men. On her left is a figure that might be named "the blind man with a staff." Painted in fluid brushstrokes very lightly charged with color, he cuts a majestic figure; his eyes half closed, he is making a gesture of mournful resignation. The grief apparent on his face suggests that he may be the saint's father, laboring under an unjust charge of murder.

Closely grouped and linked up with each other, these eight figures are the chief *dramatis personae.* The rest are mere spectators, who are reacting in very different ways to the extraordinary event they are witnessing. Some make it clear by their expressions that they are keenly interested; others wear an aloof, indifferent air, so stolid, in some cases, that they seem hardly human and make one think of moonstruck owls perched at nightfall on a belfry. They might be styled "the non-participants." Some of them are obviously vagabonds and beggars who have come here from the highroads or church porches and, for all their peaceful airs, may be planning to bring off some crime, petty or otherwise. It is amongst these predatory types—spectators plainly anxious not to betray their guilty secrets and intentions—that we find some of the boldest, most terrifying representations of the human visage that even Goya ever made. In these faces the paint is laid on in sudden, savage strokes leaving the features undefined; they call to mind the creations of Solana or Rouault and equal, indeed outdo, the most audacious distortions of modern Expressionism.

2 Behind the blind man with a staff is one of the most monumental, most happily inspired figures in the whole cupola; let us call him the Old Testament Prophet. Gazing heavenwards, he has—like Moses on Mount Horeb—his arms outspread and there is a striking contrast between the fiery gesture of this "prophet" and the attitudes of the three "Majas on the Balcony" in front of him. Obviously these three young women, busy chattering about their private concerns, could not care less about the miracle. They form an admirable trio in true Goya style. The one on the left is wearing a white mantilla and a red skirt; the girl behind her, whose features are less clearly rendered, has a dress sprinkled with touches of delicate pistachio green. The third, a bewitching houri with big dark eyes, is one of Goya's most effective, daringly conceived figures. Here the boldness of the execution, even the type of womanhood she represents, remind us of Delacroix's *Women of Algiers.*

3 If we now turn back to the north, that is to say towards the figures behind the saint, we notice at once some greatly simplified faces anticipating those in the "black paintings." So as to get a close-up view of what is happening, two children are scrambling up on to the railing; one is already astride it. Next comes a standing man with his right arm raised; we are inclined to call him the "superstitious man," since he is making the traditional gesture for warding off evil. Beside him, with his back to us, is "the man running away," a peasant type with a big hat who seems in a desperate hurry to get out of the crowd. This has led some to think that here we have the real murderer, panic-stricken at the turn of events. The way of escape is barred by two stolid-looking men whose faces are built up in separate brushstrokes, dappled with flecks of greenish blue.

4 The scene just described is prolonged into the background by two faces that are nothing short of astounding. The painter seems to have let his brush run free, splashing dabs of bright yellowish ochre upon a ground of browns and black, with an effect so startling that we can hardly believe our eyes. Bold as is the treatment of the face seen in profile, it is outdone by that beside it: a queer gorilla-like head, vaguely indicated by the gaping cavity of the mouth and black holes for the eyes. But now a change comes. Here is a well-defined, orderly group of figures far more pleasing to the eye, whom Rothe dubs "the sensitives." First we have a girl uplifting her clasped hands, thrilled by the wonder of the scene; the dominant color in this charming figure is off-white set off by carmine. The young man beside her, whose right hand is resting on the railing, seems no less moved; he is wearing a sort of "Russian smock" with wide sleeves, held in by a sash. Behind him stands a heavily built woman watching the miracle with an air of ecstasy.

second fragment

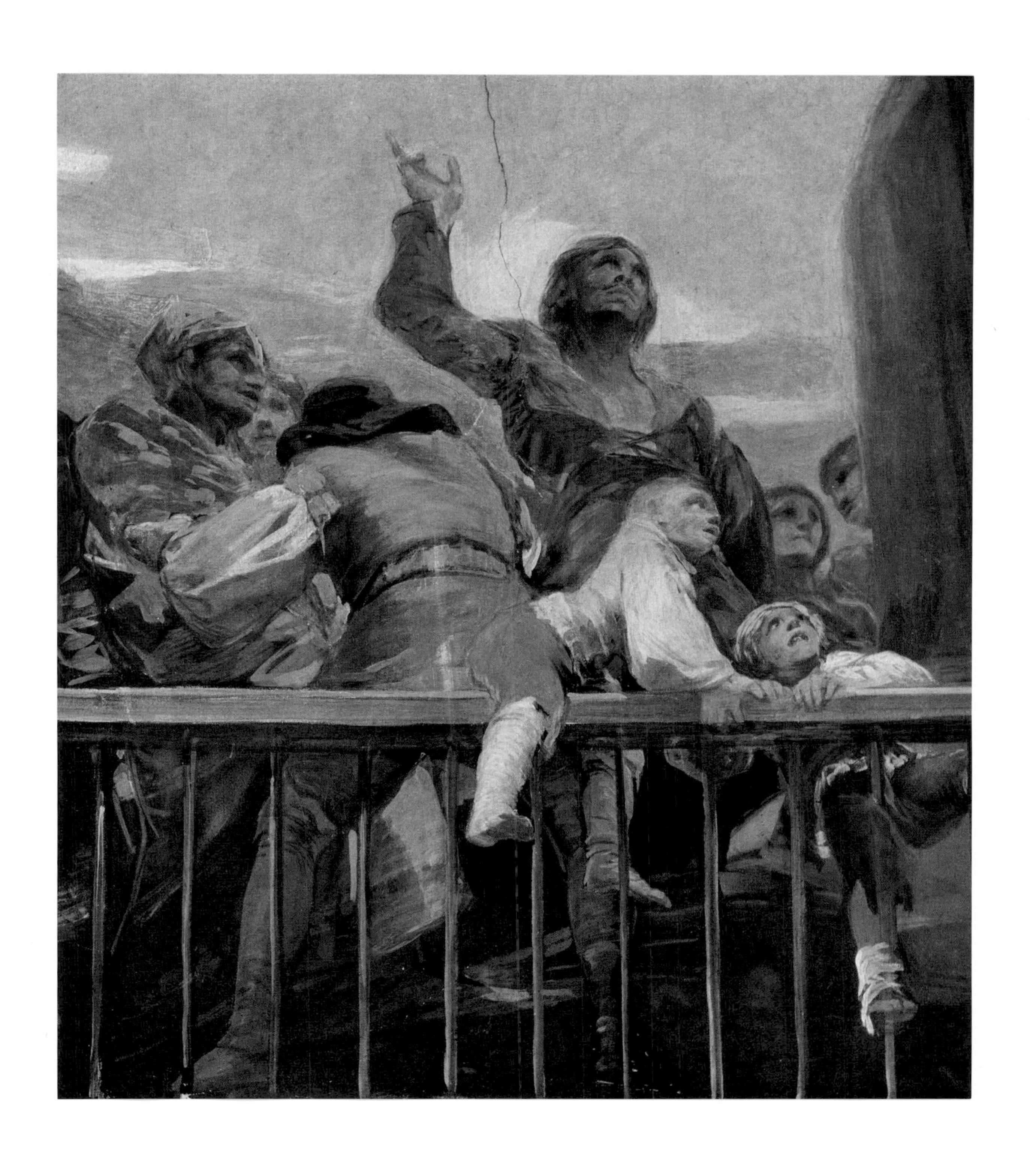

third fragment

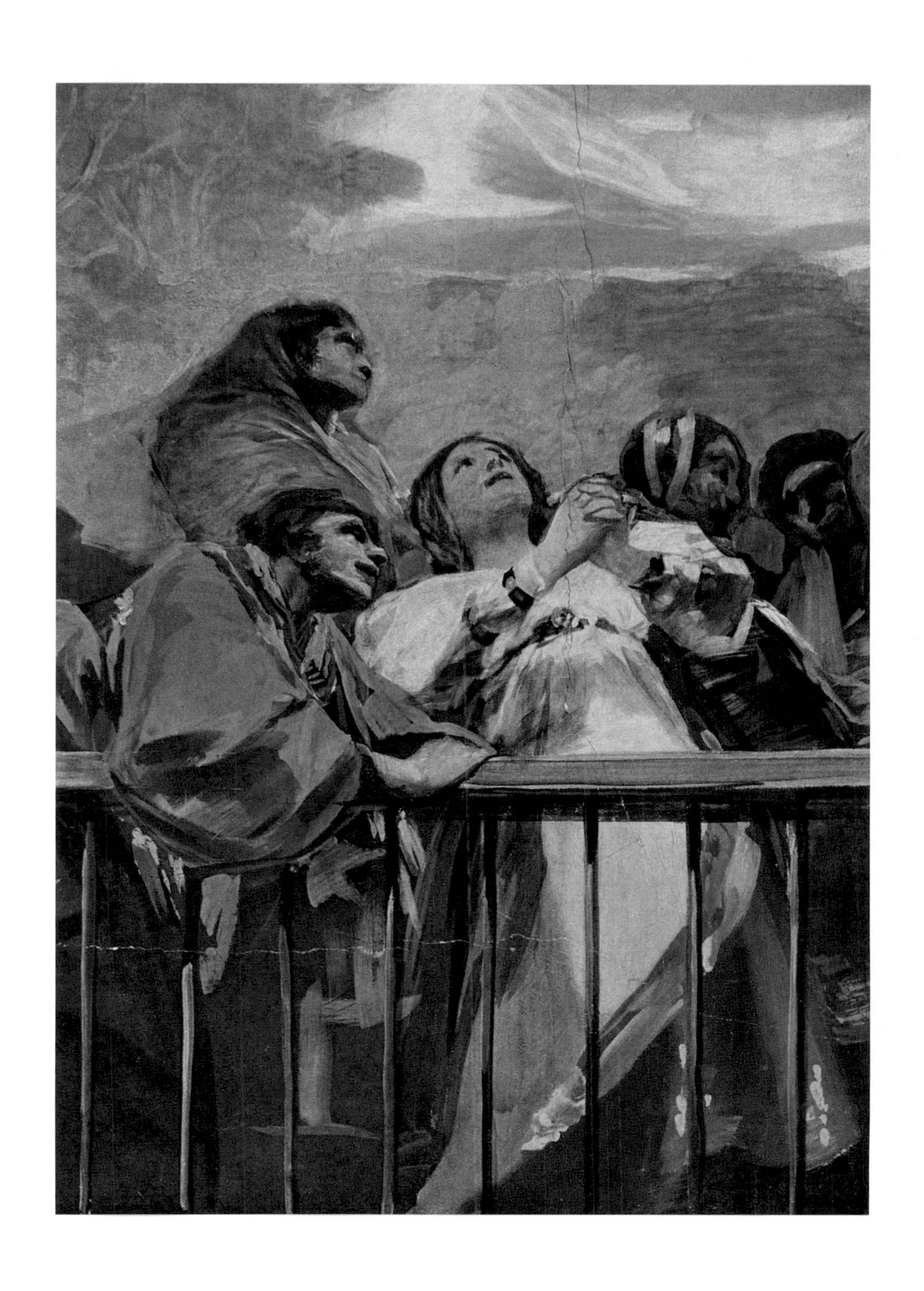

fourth fragment

Fl. 17

fifth fragment

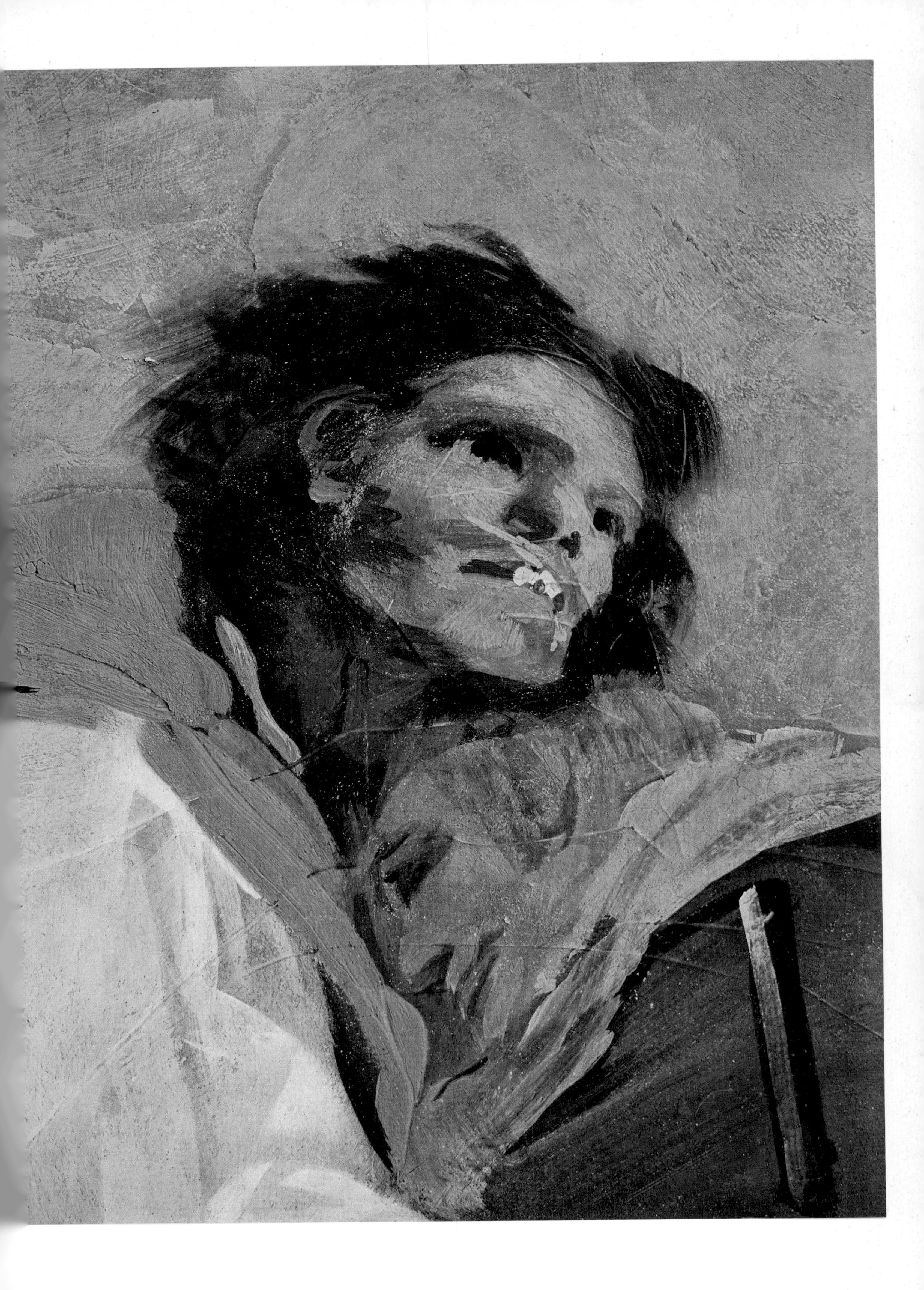

sixth fragment

seventh fragment

82 · 83

eighth fragment

THE ANGELS OF LA FLORIDA

THE other paintings in the church are hardly more than a decorative pendant to the leading theme which occupies the cupola. The cherubs and seraphs on the cornice seem to be directing the gaze of the congregation in the body of the church to the miracle which is being performed by St Anthony above their heads; their function is, in fact, that of heightening the effect—spectacular, not to say theatrical—of the ensemble. In striking contrast with the macabre fantasy of the figures in the cupola, here all is grace and beauty, sensual appeal. Angels (not in the least "androgynous" to my thinking, but frankly feminine) and naked babes with butterflies' wings are uplifting heavy curtains in gold brocade so as to reveal the miracle taking place on high. Here, too, Goya's brush has conjured up a magic world by means of color; deft touches of yellow ochre give the illusion of gold thread woven into the silky fabric of the curtains, which make an effective background to the elegantly posed angels clad in ivory-pale robes, with bands, fringes and trimmings in heavy, glistening silk of rich but sober hues: black, ochre, gold, green, blue and pink. With their graceful limbs and amply molded forms clearly perceptible beneath their garments, Goya's angels, despite their wings, are women unmistakably; indeed so mundane are their charms that one would be more inclined to take them for young persons dressed up for some gala night at court than for celestial visitants. Their arms and necks are bare, and the exquisitely rendered flesh-tints make an effective foil to the colors of the garments. They are fair-haired and, defined by emphatic slashes of the brush, their mouths have the scarlet insistence of fresh wounds. Light ripples over them and it is light, not line, that shapes their forms and reveals the modeling of the bodies standing out in strong relief against the warmly glowing curtains.

Bodies, and especially faces, are considerably foreshortened, the effect being to give their simulated proportions a convincingly natural appearance that never jars the eye. Moreover the light seems to well up from below, as if these figures were placed in front of footlights; indeed one of the most remarkable things about the frescos is the almost mathematical exactness with which Goya has gauged the impact of this light on every part, with the result that each detail shows up and, so to speak, pulls its weight, while skillfully contrasted colors produce their maximum effect. The plastic qualities of these figures, the illusion of solidity and living presences that they create, are so compelling that the spectator can hardly tear his eye away from the fragment which for the moment he is contemplating. Even when the frescos are viewed from ground-level (though this considerably reduces the emotive shock caused by the extraordinary vigor of the brushwork when we see them in close-up), we are far from exhausting their capacity to thrill us at a first visit, or even several visits, to San Antonio. In fact no true lover of painting will ever weary of feasting his eyes on the wonders of this little church, now kept in excellent repair and easily accessible thanks to the good offices of the Royal Academy of San Fernando.

Let us now examine in detail the admirable picture sequence which figures below the cupola on the vaults of the apse and transept and near the entrance—a decorative counterpoint accompanying the representation of the miracle[27]. In the vault above the choir Goya has painted a scene complete in itself, *Twelve Angels adoring the Holy Trinity*. It has been rightly said that this picture—a preliminary sketch, here reproduced, is now in the collection of the Countess of Villagonzalo, Madrid—is the most disconcerting of all the paintings in La Florida. Goya has scattered his angels about the vault at random and, in the lower part of the composition, on the right, has had recourse to that time-honored Baroque device, here clumsily employed, of including clouds upon which the angels float. Each figure, taken by itself, is charming, exquisitely rendered, but the general effect is one of confusion, due largely to the incongruous movements of the angels, who seem to be capering in the air and dancing rather than "adoring." In this fresco we find several touches of red which probably did not exist in the original but were added in repaintings made *a secco* and perhaps intended to strengthen the effect of leaping flames culminating in the symbolical triangle. But it is also possible that Goya merely wished to produce an impression of throbbing, living light in the air traversed by these figures which fill—to the point of overcrowding—the semi-dome of the apse. Amongst them are some extremely lovely feminine forms and some with a frankly pagan appeal, for example the angel on the left who is displaying a shapely bare leg; no less effective is the graceful movement of the foreshortened bust and head, bathed in liquid light. This device of painting angels in flight, with foreshortened limbs, is the only reminiscence we find here of Goya's Baroque period (there is a very similar figure in the dome of El Pilar Cathedral at Saragossa, which he decorated in 1780).

The other paintings, on the four arches supporting the cupola and in the lunettes on each side of the transept, reproduce the same motif, with some variations: that of angels holding up ponderous curtains. In the vault of the arch preceding the choir a winged figure, unmistakably a woman, is flying forward, bare-armed, her garments trailing in the air, and the effort she is making to drag aside the curtain, so as to get a view of the miracle above, is indicated in a highly realistic manner. On the right another angel, also flying, with her leg bare, is helping her, pulling the curtain from the other side. There is a wonderful variety of tonal effects in the garments of these two angels, dappled with passages of vivid red, blue and yellow. On the cornice, on either side, are other winged figures; those on the right are kneeling, raising their eyes towards the scene that is coming into view within the cupola. On the left a genuflected figure is bowing her head as if in humble veneration of the power of the saint, while standing beside her an enchantingly beautiful winged woman gazes up in wonder, her fair hair rippling on her shoulders. This is not only one of the most attractive angels, but also one of Goya's most original creations. Here, too, are occasional touches of red, notably in the garment of the angel who is flying, with her robe billowing around her.

On the vaults of the two arches of the transept we see child angels (three on the eastern, four on the western side) flying through the air, under a big curtain, like that of a theater, which they are upholding. Just above the springings, at each end of the arches, are large figures of angels. That on the east is an elegant winged being, seen in profile, with clasped hands and an air of profound meditation. She (for there is no question of her sex) is wearing the costume Goya, so to say, standardized for his angels in this church, but here he has added two broad ribbons of golden ochre, black and a very low-keyed green. Behind this figure is a gold-brocaded fabric decorated with a large escutcheon—the Spanish royal coat of arms—seemingly embroidered on the tissue. Opposite, a winsome young angel is gazing heavenwards, with a hand to her lips and her left leg moved slightly forward. An indefinable charm emanates from this graceful figure, especially when the morning light falling on the wall brings out to the full its tactile values.

Under the arch on each side of the window is a winged figure. That on the left is one of Goya's happiest creations, such are its strangely pagan glamour and the wonderful serenity of the gaze. This figure is imbued with the neo-classical spirit and we might well believe that Goya here set out to paint an "Apollo Musagetes." Indeed the elegantly molded features and the otherworldly tranquillity of this gracious figure are reminiscent of Greek art, and this effect is heightened by a garland of flowers adorned with blue ribbons crowning the lovely head. Though the face is quite impassive, the young angel's lips are parted, as though in spellbound contemplation of some far-off vision, and the full-face presentation contributes to the atmosphere of calm. With her right hand pressed to her breast she seems to be holding up the pink bands of her tunic. The figure on the right is no less attractive and the flooding light brings out the modeling of the face and arms to wonderful effect.

On the vault of the arch to the west of the transept are four naked cherubs (two in the center and one on each side) holding up the curtains; and on the springings at each extremity a winged woman. The one on the left is wearing a reddish sash over a richly patterned dress and gazing up in ecstasy, her arms outspread; the one nearest the choir, shown in profile, has clasped her hands in prayer.

In the lunette left of the window is a woman with enormous wings and a broad sash over her bell-shaped skirt; while she lifts an arm towards the curtain she is turning her head towards the spectator, so that we see her full face. With her high coiffure, bright eyes, small short nose and girlish lips, she has a curious appeal; indeed the round head, charming features and suavely molded arms make us think of Renoir's women. The dominant note in her costume is the huge greenish sash. The winged figure on the right is rather smaller than the others, she has a frail, almost childish body, and it seems to be an effort for her to raise the heavy curtain. She is wearing a pink sash and a sort of apron of a greenish hue.

The intrados of the arch nearest the entrance has at its summit the elegantly disposed figures of two angels with their heads touching. They are flying, and their garments, picked out with touches of red and ochre and floating in the air, tell out against a background of curtains looped up on each side. On the right are two standing angels, and on the left two other angels, one of whom is on her knees. Unfortunately the group on the west side, one of the finest and most vigorous compositions in the entire church, was much damaged during the Civil War by the smoke from fires lit under it. This is all the more to be regretted since until 1936 this particular portion of the decorations had remained in exceptionally good condition. The most that could be done in the way of restoration was to clean off the dirt, and what remains is a mere shadow of this admirable piece of painting. The color has almost completely vanished and only the outlines of the figures can still be seen. To get an idea of the beauty of this group we must have recourse to the excellent etching made by José María Galván, which figures in a book to which we shall have occasion to refer at a later page.

Lastly, in the four pendentives which link the arches with the cupola, we see groups of plump little babes seated or reclining on thick cushions with golden braids and fringes. They are looking up at the vault or trying to shore up heavy curtains that are tumbling on to their heads. In these figures Goya gives us boldly foreshortened, highly personal versions of Tiepolo's cherubs.

It is hoped that this description will have given our readers a desire to visit the little church on the banks of the Manzanares and to enjoy *in situ* the beauties of the marvelous decorations it contains. Particularly striking (as can be seen from our color plates) is the way in which the leaden-grey background at the summit of the cupola brings out the white of the women's mantillas and the passages of red, less frequent but sometimes forming large patches of color in their skirts or mantles. Here and there are touches of salmon-pink, pale green and indigo, and these are present not only in garments, headdresses and ribbons, but also in faint indications of the sky above the mountains. Goya has employed a remarkable variety of ochres, ranging from bright yellow to a dusky brown. In the angels below the cupola we have patches of golden ochre, warm black and a very delicate green (on wings and garments); also, here and there, touches of pale blue. Repaintings in red can be detected chiefly in the angels flying in the vaults above the choir and near the entrance of the church. To conclude—we have here a color-scheme at once subtle and highly personal, which owed nothing to Baroque tradition or to the art of Tiepolo's immediate successors; Goya's color-orchestration in the La Florida church was as original as it is entrancing to the modern eye.

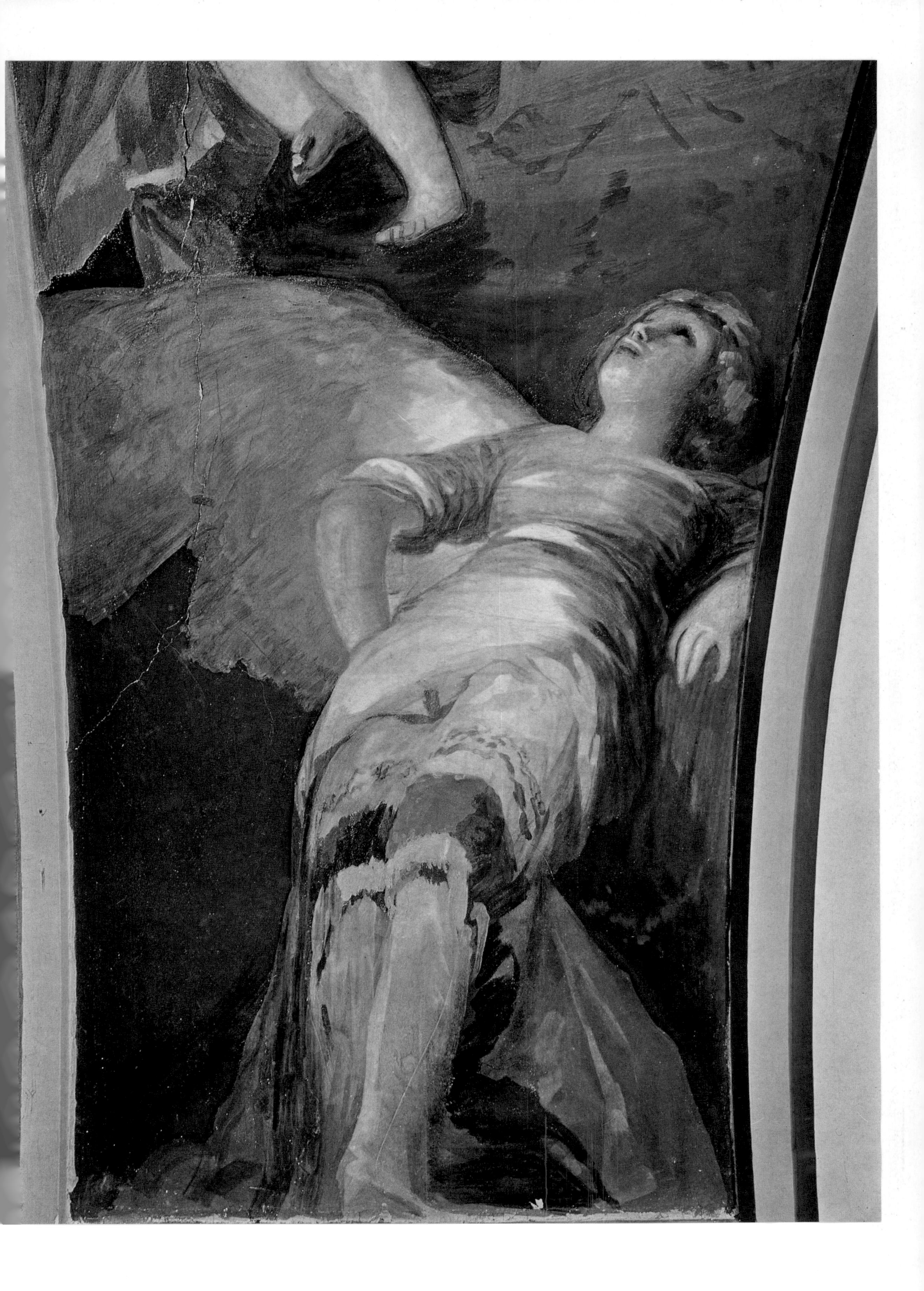

THE MIRACLE OF ST ANTHONY. SKETCH IN OILS. (10¼×15″)
COLLECTION OF THE COUNTESS OF VILLAGONZALO, MADRID.

THE PRELIMINARY SKETCHES

GOYA probably received the commission for the frescos between March 22, 1798, the date of the petition already referred to, and June 15 when his colorman delivered the first supplies. The itemized account of the latter also includes the use of the carriage that drove Goya to the church and afterwards took him home, to No. 1, Calle del Desengaño; charges for the carriage came to fifty-two reals per day. According to the invoice it was used every day without a break from August 1 until the work was finished [28], which gives a total of 120 days. Personally, I find it difficult to believe Goya took so long, even granting that the number of separate wall surfaces he had to paint in different parts of the church may have slowed down the work to some extent, since the scaffolding had to be re-erected each time he moved from one part of the building to another. Moreover, what we know of Goya's previous fresco-painting justifies us in accepting this itemized account with some reserve. Presumably Goya used the carriage now and then for private purposes, and even if we assume he visited the church daily, this may merely have been to keep an eye on things and to see how the plaster was setting.

According to Father Tomás López, a monk at the Carthusian monastery of Aula Dei and a contemporary of Goya, the artist took only forty days to paint a surface of 250 square yards in the cupola of the Cathedral of El Pilar at Saragossa—which means that he then progressed at the rate of five or six square yards a day [29]. However, we must bear in mind the fact that Goya's health had been badly shaken shortly before he started on the San Antonio frescos and no doubt he had to be careful not to overtire himself. Even so, however, I feel that the bill for materials supplied and the 6,240 reals of carriage charges are not to be taken too seriously. In the technical analysis of the frescos which appears later in this volume, Professor Stolz points ironically to the quite preposterous quantity of materials Goya ordered—at the king's expense, needless to say—for the work at La Florida; far more than he could possibly have employed on these frescos. The most ordinary colors are itemized in batches of a half arroba (about thirteen pounds), and brushes and pots by the dozen! In fact Goya multiplied his requirements all along the line, and he probably did much the same thing where the carriage was concerned.

After familiarizing himself with the story of the miracle in *The Christian Year*, Goya made some preliminary sketches. I have particularly in mind the two small studies now in the collection of the Countess of Villagonzalo, in Madrid, who has very kindly granted permission, for the first time, for their reproduction in color; hence their presence in this volume. These are (following Goya's usual practice) no more than rough sketches, hasty jottings-down of ideas, intended simply to map out the main lines of the composition without going into details. The first represents the miracle scene; already outlined in it are the group surrounding the man raised from the dead, the balustrade, the man flinging up his arms, the youngster clambering on to the railing, and the big drape hung in a semicircle over it. On comparing this with the finished work, we see that some very important changes have been made. The main figure group has been simplified, and an overcrowded secondary group on the right suppressed altogether; in other words, as so often happens with Goya, the lay-out has been vastly improved at the last minute. The landscape also has been changed a good deal, but the most important innovation is the suppression of the angels which, in the preliminary sketch, were shown hovering above the central scene.

This last modification is the most revealing of all, since it proves that Goya's first impulse was to hark back to the lay-out employed in his previous frescos, and even to Baroque procedures. But he pulled himself up in time and the significance of this change of program can hardly be over-estimated [30]. After that momentary lapse—and how much it has to tell us!—he resolved to strike out in a wholly new direction. It was now no doubt that the idea occurred to him of relegating the angels to the lower portions of the church. And, having broken with tradition once for all, he felt no scruples about innovating still further in the depiction of those heavenly beings. The result was a bevy of charmingly feminine angels who remind us sometimes of Renoir's appetizing young women, sometimes of classical flower-garlanded figures of Apollo, sometimes of pretty chorus-girls fluttering across the stage in all their frills and furbelows. The sketch for *The Miracle of St Anthony*, brushed in rapidly on a reddish ground, has none of the elaborateness of the preliminary studies made for his early frescos. This says much for the self-confidence with which Goya embarked on the decoration of San Antonio; he knew exactly what he was to do [31].

Outlined and colored even more lightly than the first, the second sketch is a delightfully fresh and vivid study in bright hues on a very pale ground, on which the dark forms of the angels stand out, painted with the tip of the brush and enlivened with dainty touches of blue, red and pink. This sketch, too, differs very greatly from the finished work, which in this case, unfortunately, failed to retain the charm of the original color harmonies and the grouping of the figures. Had Goya kept faithfully to the preliminary sketch, the angels would perhaps have seemed too small, almost insignificant; by bringing them more to the front, he enlarged the scale of the figures, with the result that he had to bunch them together, and in the process sacrificed the delightfully vivacious rhythm imparted to the angels in the sketch. Other preparatory studies have been referred to by various writers. I have no knowledge of those mentioned by Mayer some years ago as being privately owned in England; all trace of them seems to have been lost [32]. As for the small picture in the Lazaro Galdiano Museum, Madrid, on the other hand, I must confess that I cannot accept it as genuine; the technique as a whole and various details suggest it to be a sketch in the Goya manner by an imitator, probably one of the Lucas group of painters. Not by Goya either are the drawings in the former Castillo Olivares Collection published by Rothe; in my opinion, they may very possibly be the work of Eugenio Lucas himself [33].

I think it unlikely that Goya used any help in the actual painting of the San Antonio frescos. True, this type of work usually requires a team of assistants, but their duties are limited to the preparation and mixing of the colors. In Goya's case, given the way he worked, impetuously, at the prompting of his instinct, we can hardly imagine his employing an assistant, except for these purely menial tasks; indeed the employment of such "understudies" is only possible when the master has prepared in advance fully detailed

ANGELS ADORING THE TRINITY. SKETCH IN OILS. (10¼ × 15″)
COLLECTION OF THE COUNTESS OF VILLAGONZALO, MADRID.

cartoons exactly the same size as the projected work. Unlike most fresco-painters, Goya, it seems, never made any cartoons; anyhow none have come to light. This, of course, does not rule out the possibility that he may have employed an assistant to color the backgrounds or, as Professor Stolz thinks likely, to retouch in tempera the joints between portions of the wall painted on successive days.

Since Carderera's time, the only painter mentioned as being Goya's disciple is the Valencian Asensio Juliá, of whom the master made two portraits; one of them, formerly in the collection of the Dukes of Montpensier, is now in the United States, in the Paul Sachs Collection. Actually, however, there is some doubt as to whether this is really one of Juliá, the exact wording of its inscription being a moot point. Mayer's reading is "*Goya a su amigo Asensio*" [34]; others think the name should be read "Asensi." Goya is known to have made the portrait of a certain Don Tomás Asensi, but I have no knowledge of its present whereabouts [35]. One thing, however, is certain: the portrait in the Sachs Collection shows a man standing on a scaffolding in the working clothes of a fresco-painter with pots of paint beside him [36] and if this man is really to be identified as Juliá, it supports the view that it was he who acted as Goya's assistant. Juliá is thought to have been born in 1767, though some sources say 1748. The latter date would make him an almost exact contemporary of Goya; but if the birthdate of 1767 is correct, Juliá would have been a man of thirty-one in 1798 when Goya painted the San Antonio frescos, and this seems to be about the age of the man in the Sachs portrait.

There is more certainty about the identity of the man in the second portrait, which used to be in the Madrazo Collection and which Mayer mentioned in 1925 as being in England [37]. I have never seen the picture but there are no two opinions as to the inscription on it: *A Don Sensio* [sic] *Juliá su amigo Por Goya 1814*." Nor can there be any doubt that Juliá's known works show traces of Goya's influence.

THE NATURE OF GOYA'S ART

ALTHOUGH the San Antonio frescos were not the culminating point of Goya's career as a mural painter—which was to have a dramatic climax many years later in the "black paintings" of the Quinta del Sordo—they were his supreme and last achievement in the field of the fresco proper. It is obvious that in San Antonio he had a heaven-sent opportunity for painting exactly as he wished, without any of the irritating restrictions he had to endure at Saragossa in 1780. All his life long Goya was spurred on by his fiery temperament, an urge to express himself fully and without restraint. Like a thoroughbred he loathed the feeling of being curbed and was for ever seeking new outlets for his torrential energy. This desire for freedom and independence, in his life and in his art, was ever with him while he was following the tedious path of his official career. "If only I had nothing to put up with from anyone!" he wrote, in 1783 or thereabouts, to his friend Zapater.

There are also references to the envy and incomprehension of his fellow artists, Mengs' all-too-willing satellites, in Goya's letters to his Saragossa friend. Writing in 1788 he complained bitterly of never having time to do the sort of work he liked. During his convalescence, however, when he was not obliged to work to order or to perform any official duties, he could devote himself to "creations of the imagination" in which "invention and caprice were given free rein." Thus at long last, conscious of the maturity of his talent and freed from the handicaps of youth, Goya could follow the promptings of his own indomitable will; could turn his back on the painting of his epoch, his colleagues' superstitious dread of "breaking the rules," their cult of the *beau idéal* and all the far-fetched notions that Mengs had promoted to the rank of dogmas, sacrosanct and—for the artist—soporific. True, the order for the work at La Florida came from the king, but Goya was to carry it out alone, without any outside interference. And, in any case, this was only a small chapel for the use of employees of the Royal Patrimony and the Customs. Here, anyhow, he could take risks, and how happily he took them!

As though to signalize his break with tradition and all it stood for, Goya deliberately inverted the lay-out normally employed in the decoration of church domes. The Baroque artists had filled them with depictions of the heavens opening in a great burst of light, with flying forms hovering at the summit of the dome and celestial beings borne on fleecy clouds, rendered with all the illusionist effects of foreshortening and perspective. This was what Goya himself had done in the Cathedral of El Pilar, where he remained faithful to Baroque tradition in his compositional scheme, though in the execution he took some liberties. In La Florida we have a wholly different world; here, on his own initiative, Goya rejected, lock, stock and barrel, all those overworked devices. And, in defiance of all logic, he placed the terrestrial portion of the scene—the miracle performed by the saint—high up in the cupola and relegated the supramundane elements, angels, seraphs and cherubs, to lower registers, below the cornice. (It is true, however, that he gave the latter a quite startlingly mundane appearance—which lessens the paradoxical effect of this arrangement—and that their function is simply that of holding up the heavy fabric of a celestial stage-curtain so as to reveal to us the miracle taking place overhead.) Another interesting innovation is that *The Adoration of the Trinity*, whose place would normally have been in the cupola, where it would have given an opportunity for the presentation, in the Correggio manner, of concentric rings of angels floating on buoyant clouds, is located in the apse, *below* the level of the miracle.

Goya's intention was to delight the eye of the visitor to the church with a relatively close-up view of charming, butterfly-winged babes and fair-haired, winsome angels. In the scene of the miracle, on the other hand, he aimed at an effect of remoteness, taking advantage of the height at which it was placed and the attenuated light that fell on it from the "lantern" windows. In this scene, anyhow, he could indulge to his heart's content in the kind of brushwork he enjoyed, rapid and spontaneous. Not a trace remains of the anecdotal iconography of the past, and in this connection a penetrating observation by Malraux may be cited: "Goya's painting is a law unto itself; many great artists had already had glimpses of that law but none had dared to voice it openly. That law is, briefly: (1) the primacy of the specific means of painting over those of representation and (2) the artist's right to draw and paint not with a view to creating an illusion and depicting a given scene with the utmost possible convincingness, but to express himself."

The nature of genius cannot be defined but we can trace its course, and Goya's is revealed most clearly in the wholly personal evolution of his art and the way in which he sought and found his own solutions to art's problems, solutions undreamt-of by any of his contemporaries. Let us not forget that Goya lived in the heyday of the neo-classical movement and belonged to the same generation as Jacques-Louis David, Asmus Carstens and John Flaxman, who all alike, swimming with the current of the age, pinned their faith to a revival, sometimes on rather naïve lines, of the art of classical antiquity. Everything was in favor of such a program; this was the time when archeologists were busily uncovering the buried secrets of the past, the era of the great discoveries at Herculaneum and the publication of large albums of engravings illustrating ancient monuments. The neo-classical artist was all for meticulous drawing and the definition of form by well-marked contour-lines; he had an instinctive, puritanical distaste for the charms of color. All these men (amongst them Mengs, with whom Goya was in close contact) specialized in smooth, immaculate brushwork, glossy surfaces and conventional nudes approximating as nearly as might be to Greek statues or their Roman copies. Thus, set against the background of his age, Goya cuts the figure of a solitary genius. Yet he did not start out from nothing; he had had a solid apprenticeship in art and his capacity for assimilation was exceptional.

This is not the place, however, to go into the early influences that shaped Goya's art; I have discussed these elsewhere [38]. Moving counter to the trend of his age and revealing in his pictures a new way of seeing, Goya built up an œuvre rich in intimations for the future and mapped out the path—or, rather, many of the paths, and those the boldest—that western painting was to follow in the 19th and 20th centuries. Discarding classical line, he realized his vision in terms of light and color; turning his back on the mannered, somewhat mawkish art in favor with most 18th-century painters, he struck down to the roots of life and, reacting against the discreetly modulated painting then in fashion, developed a vigorous technique of his own, all in slashing brushstrokes and expressive touches that instantly recorded his visual and emotional experiences. Above all, Goya was mindful of the over-all unity of the picture, its tonality, and rendered form and volumes by means of contrasting touches at a time when other painters were cultivating, almost *ad nauseam*, paucity of statement and a finicking perfection. The violence of the execution in the pictures he was free to paint as he wished and into which he put his heart helps us to understand his pessimistic outlook, that rankling discontent which was the outcome of the successive "crises" of his life.

This embittered vision reveals itself most clearly in one of the procedures which most of all affiliates Goya to our modern sensibility: the ruthless, not to say brutal distortions he imposes on forms and figures; sometimes even in his portraits. Goya's break with the past, notably in the La Florida cupola, took two forms. First, he brought to an end (unwittingly, no doubt) the traditional, humanistic attitude to art, transmitted by Baroque, which stood for classical values and the glorification of Man. According to this view, art's function was to sublimate Man above the human condition and its ignominies and exhibit him made perfect: the hero triumphant over the frailties flesh is heir to, and all that might degrade him. Goya (and following him all modern art) rejects this flattering illusion and explores the soul of man, without the least attempt to beautify what he discovers; on the contrary, he reveals in all its ugliness the diabolic streak inherent in the human personality. In Goya's work the hero-man of Renaissance and Baroque art becomes man the victim of his fate, at the mercy of passions making him ridiculous, a grotesque puppet in the hands of ironical Olympians. His theatrical handling of narrative subjects, his practice of staging each scene as though lit up by footlights, rises at La Florida—as at Santa Cueva (Cadiz) and in the "black paintings" of the Quinta del Sordo—far above the anecdotal or the picturesque, and attains an emotive power unique in art.

"In Goya's art," writes Malraux, "we have not light but only *lighting*"—lighting as used in the theater. This lighting brings out the very essence of reality, and its magic creates an ambiance in which forms acquire that plastic immediacy which is the painter's real "subject." In fact Goya—to quote Malraux again—"tends not to evoke any given space but to conjure up forms out of shadows." The technical study by Professor Stolz included in this volume, strictly objective as it is, does not belie this apt observation. It explains why Goya often gives his figures such curiously unsubstantial backgrounds and this view is borne out by Gómez Moreno's study [39] of the backgrounds of Goya's pictures. Actually, however, Goya's treatment of backgrounds falls in line with the general practice of the Spanish school. The playing-down of space so as to stress what Pacheco and 17th-century writers call "relief" derives from the "sculptural instinct" [40] which Oscar Hagen has described as one of the constants of our painting and of Spanish aesthetic as a whole. Such painting gives priority to the representation of volumes and invokes, above all, our sense of tactile values. What, one is inclined to wonder, is the true purport of that array of impassive or seemingly hypnotized faces stamped by Goya's brush with the imprint of an ineluctable destiny; faces void of any aspirations towards bliss or beauty and, on the contrary, promised to corruption and death? Here again one of Malraux's brilliant intuitions provides an answer. "Goya is guided by an instinctive belief that the whole religious sense—for, though we may not like to admit it, whatever is opposed to beauty is in the last analysis the sacrosanct—rests on the awareness of another world." But here we come up against a terrible limitation, or, if we prefer to call it so, a malady of modern life. Man is ceasing (as Goya foresaw intuitively) to be able to envisage the sacrosanct as a vision of supernatural beauty; he is beginning to sense, like Goya in his glimpses of a world of weird hallucinations, witches and phantoms—the monstrous brood that comes to life "when Reason sleeps"—the horror and the helplessness of the human situation when man confronts, unaided and alone, the unfathomable mysteries of the universe. This is why we must agree with Malraux that Goya's genius lay "not only in his having broken with harmony and chosen horror, but also in his discovery of a style analogous to the great religious styles." Inevitably western man, who since the 18th century has been trying to dispense with God, is led to seek for a substitute for Faith—an emotion consoling him for his own insignificance and futility. He finds it, like Faust, in scientific research into the scheme of things; or in the exploration by other means of the ghoul-haunted jungle of man's secret self; or in the constructions of social or political systems capable of filling the space left empty on the pedestals of his fallen gods; or else in the bleak despair of philosophic negativism. In short, he devotes himself to feverish attempts to find a personal explanation of the world, attempts which, depriving him of the comforts of religion, can but isolate him and lead him into the wilderness.

Secondly, we would draw attention to something of prime importance to all modern art that Goya was the first to formulate: a profound dissociation between the painted subject and the actual painting, the execution. It is clear that nowadays, for better or for worse, what rouses our aesthetic emotion and supplies the "thrill" we seek for in the work of art is the artist's plastic language, not any sentimental appeal in the subject; we no longer regard the artistic form in which the latter is expressed as a means to an end and nothing more. Not that I wish to suggest that this contemporary aesthetic is the best of all possible aesthetics; all that can be said is that for the present it holds the field without a rival. This is why Goya made short work of all the principles of humanistic art and the idealism of Mengs and his associates. At one swoop he destroyed the superstitious cult of fidelity to nature and the model and conscientious reproduction of the forms "given" by Nature.

All this is fully borne out by the frescos in the cupola. Some may read into them no more than an arbitrary transcription of everyday street scenes, a vivid "slice of life" straight from the Madrid of Goya's day. Others may try to convince us that Goya's sole aim was to illustrate the religious theme assigned him to the best of his ability, and that, in his own way, he achieved this aim. But what cannot be denied is that, whatever elements of contemporary life he may have based his work on, and whatever anecdote he made the starting-point of his composition, these were no more than the raw material which, in his hands, underwent one of those strange metamorphoses that are the miracles of art. Here both reality and iconography are sublimated, lifted on to another plane, not merely that of painting pure and simple, but one in which each figure represented is shown as he essentially is, confronted by the tragic, terrifying reality of the human predicament. These people are denizens of a dark limbo or purgatory, but a purgatory without hope of salvation in the end. Even the personages who are deeply moved seem not so much affected by religious emotion or any spiritual rapture, but relegated to a state of humble acquiescence in their lot. Others strike us as completely indifferent, self-centered, irrelevant to the central theme—though each figure is a superb piece of painting in itself. Their faces seem petrified in a grimace, like masks that reveal character by overstatement and caricature. "For Goya," writes André Malraux, "a mask is not what hides a face but what defines it."

The most striking thing about these paintings, however, is the marvelous variety of attitudes. This, to my mind (rather than the iconographical ambiguity in their presentation), is the source of that exquisite glow of femininity which, like a subtle perfume, envelops all the winged beings in the church. Goya understands woman; he brings out all the natural grace of her attitudes and gestures at their delightful best; hence the glamour of these angels, and their incomparable charm. Such are the elegance and the rhythm the artist has imparted to the movements and postures of these young women that some have said these angels are Spanish *majas* and nothing else. And indeed, whether Goya intended this or not, the way they stand, turn their heads, move their arms and hands, leaves no doubt as to their kinship with the young women in his portraits and tapestry cartoons. There is in fact a family likeness between all Goya's women, for the good reason that he employs for them a repertory of gestures and attitudes taken straight from life. Their distinctive qualities are poise and style. With the suave dignity, the fine bearing of Spanish women and in particular those of Madrid, he was naturally familiar; but the style he created for himself. And to the style are due the many similarities between the *ángelas* of San Antonio and the *majas* and *manolas* of his non-religious paintings.

GOYA'S METHODS OF WORK

UNTIL 1910 none of the books dealing with Goya's work gave any adequate account of the frescos at San Antonio de la Florida. In the second volume of his study of Goya, *Composiciones y figuras,* Aureliano de Beruete implied he was about to say the last word on the subject when he began his chapter on them thus: "We must examine closely these paintings in San Antonio de la Florida, on which so many hasty, not to say erroneous opinions have been expressed." However this "close" examination did not prevent Beruete from falling into errors of his own. For instance when he self-confidently says: "We can be sure of our ground when we point out that not all the composition was executed in the true fresco technique; and if this is so, it follows that Goya made use of tempera, an opaque medium producing a mat surface of a delicate texture; easy to manipulate, it is suitable for covering large areas since it dries quicker than other media, leaving the brushstrokes clearly visible."

We may begin by pointing out that Beruete based his conclusions more on inferences than on actual observation—always a dangerous practice where works of art are concerned. Here is an example. In the list of supplies delivered to Goya for the San Antonio frescos we find an item: "1¾ lbs of washed sponges." Commenting on this entry he boldly declares that "these sponges reveal the secret of the very special technique employed by Goya in this work." According to him, Goya began by lightly rubbing with sponges soaked in the appropriate color those portions of the wall where the darker masses were to be placed, then painted in the rest in tempera on this more or less monochrome ground. It is to be regretted that Beruete's theory, ingenious but ill-advised, met with such wide acceptance. For a close-up examination of the paintings in a good light reveals that it was very wide of the mark. Needless to say, the fault lay not with Beruete nor with the painters and critics who followed his lead; neither he nor they had the good fortune we have had of seeing the paintings under the most favorable conditions.

But there may also be another explanation. Such was the predominance of easel-painting and the oil medium in the 19th century that most painters had only the vaguest ideas about fresco technique. Artists and critics alike were unaware of certain elementary facts with which the merest tyro had been familiar in earlier days. Towards the close of the 19th century, however—particularly in France, after the rise of Divisionism—problems of technique became the artists' chief concern and they sought to enlarge their means of expression by careful study of the methods of the old masters. None the less, as recently as forty years ago many artists still spoke of fresco-painting as a secret technique, shrouded in mystery, and I remember having heard a painter, just back from Italy, declaring in all seriousness, that he had been initiated into fresco-painting by an aged teacher who "still remembered" the secrets of the masters! On this point the opinion expressed by that eminent authority on art and on fresco-painting in particular, Ramón Stolz, in the appendix to this volume is conclusive, when he points out that there can be no "mystery" about a technique whose every element is so clearly to be seen.

Happily things are very different today. Many contemporary artists have a thorough knowledge of the technical side of painting and, what is more, they have at their disposal scientific analyses, made by experts, of the colors used by the old masters. What baffles our art critics and so many others, painters included, when they examine Goya's frescos, particularly those in San Antonio, is that, though he used the ordinary techniques, he handled them in a quite original and unexpected manner, with the result that while the means were traditional, the work looks wholly modern.

Commenting on the San Antonio frescos, Eugenio d'Ors, with a certain shrewdness but in the somewhat disparaging tone he thinks fit to adopt when speaking of this artist, remarks that "Goya did not take his task over-seriously; he was not going to be bothered with the long and arduous spells of work that true fresco technique calls for, when painting this 'suburban chapel."' Certainly it is quite possible that if Goya took such liberties in painting the San Antonio frescos, this was because he did not expect they would greatly affect his reputation one way or the other [41], and his sense of relative irresponsibility encouraged him to boldness. Also, now that Bayeu was dead and Mengs a "back number," there was no risk of being taken to task by champions of the *beau idéal*. But where d'Ors goes astray is when he so blithely endorses what might be called the sponge-and-tempera theory. Indeed, judging by the tone in which he writes we can see he hardly takes the matter seriously. "Goya began by buying several dozen sponges and a basin. Next he mixed his pigments in the basin and applied them on the wall with the sponges. Is this fresco painting? Or tempera? There are even brushstrokes done in oils. No word exists that I know of to describe this medley of techniques" [42]. All that was needed was a scaffolding and a close-up study of the paintings, and these ingenious hypotheses collapsed like a pricked bubble.

Some years ago, however, José López Rey published in the Gazette des Beaux-Arts [43] a sensible, well-considered article on the San Antonio frescos. Though he had not had an opportunity of examining them when they were cleaned after the Civil War, a careful, analytical study of the list of materials supplied by Goya's colorman—that selfsame list which had so much misled Beruete—led him to conclusions which have been proved correct. López Rey compared this list with the chapter, regarded by Spanish painters as the *locus classicus* on the subject, which Palomino devoted to the technique of fresco-painting, and this comparison proved that Goya kept strictly to the methods prescribed by Palomino. López Rey reached in fact the same conclusions as those of Stolz after he had studied *in situ* the frescos in El Pilar and San Antonio. In the much-discussed list of supplies discovered in the archives of the Royal Palace to which reference has already been made, we find that the following colors were bought by the "half arroba" (i.e. 13 lbs): dark ochre, crimson, black earth, red earth, Venetian umber, green clay and fine umber. These were evidently to be the ground colors of the projected work. Amongst the other pigments, bought in smaller quantities, and presumably to be used more sparingly, are: light yellow, Chinese vermilion, flower of indigo, Molina blue, superfine London carmine, smalt and English blue. Most of these colors, light yellow and crimson included, figure among those described by Palomino as "indispensable" for fresco-painting [44].

Palomino—who was born at Bujalance, near Cordova, in 1653 and died in 1726—was the author of a famous treatise on painting widely read in Goya's time and thought highly of by Spanish painters. This work, *El Museo pictórico y escala óptica* (Madrid, 1715-1724), was a compendium of the oral traditions of Spanish art in their purest form. Himself a practising artist, Palomino continued painting frescos in the technique which had made good in Madrid during the 17th century under the auspices of Juan Carreño, Francisco Rizi and Claudio Coello, and was justified in regarding himself as a direct heir of the great Baroque master Luca Giordano who had decorated to such brilliant effect so many churches and so many ceilings in Spanish palaces. An exceedingly prolific fresco-painter, Palomino had had much experience and knew his subject-matter well. We must also remember that, before his journey to Italy (where he probably made a point of acquainting himself with fresco technique), Goya had studied under José Luzán, who had been a pupil (at Naples) of Mastroleo and could thus regard himself as being in the same tradition as Giordano. There is no reason to believe that, apart from this well-defined succession of influences, the practice of fresco-painting had undergone any modification between the publication of Palomino's treatise and the time when Goya was studying under Luzán. Thus López Rey's conclusions are well founded; Goya kept closely to the traditional Baroque technique, which then prevailed all over Europe and is set forth in detail by Antonio Palomino. In this context we may cite a short passage in Palomino's treatise which seems singularly appropriate to our artist. The fresco technique, he says, "is unsuited to timid painters, to copyists and all who tend to seek inspiration from others." The fresco-painter, he continues, should "follow his own inspiration, thus only can he ensure the freedom, full control of his materials and powerful effects called for by this kind of painting." To what painter could these remarks better apply than to Goya?

There can be no doubt that, like all artists of his day, Goya had a copy of the *Museo pictórico* in his studio and often consulted it. López Rey aptly reminds us that when in 1783, fifteen years before the San Antonio frescos, Goya made his "official" portrait of the Count of Floridablanca, then chief minister of state, whose patronage meant so much to him in those early days, he was careful to include in the picture tokens of his patron's interest in the arts: ground plans, compasses and folio volumes; and that amongst the latter was a book bound in vellum, lying on the ground and placed in such a way that its title could easily be read—and this book was Palomino's *Práctica de la Pintura,* second volume of his *magnum opus.* Thus it is clear that even as a quite young man Goya was familiar with this work, as indeed was to be expected.

When, after the ending of the Civil War, the San Antonio paintings were being restored, they were carefully examined by Ramón Stolz. Both Stolz and myself are enthusiastic admirers of Goya's art, and the scaffolding set up for the restoration of the paintings enabled us to study them at leisure and to examine their texture. Stolz told me then and there he was absolutely convinced that these were frescos done in the true *buon fresco* technique. In the course of our frequent conversations on the subject, he often reverted to this point, backing his view with arguments which, coming from one endowed with such keen powers of observation and so wide a knowledge of the traditional color techniques of the masters, carried entire conviction. It is always distasteful to the art historian having to refute, as categorically as I here am doing, the views of an eminent predecessor—of several predecessors in the present case. But though by and large my respect for Beruete and his achievements as a critic and writer has not diminished, I feel it my duty to draw attention to the errors into which he fell when dealing with the San Antonio frescos.

One of the most irritating forms of pedantry is that of the art critic who though he has no practical experience of painting lays down the law in matters of pure technique, under the impression that it is enough to have read widely on the subject. For this reason I welcome the enlightened collaboration of Professor Stolz and am glad to include his article on the technique employed by Goya at San Antonio de la Florida. None is better qualified than he in this respect since, having restored the Goya frescos in the Cathedral of El Pilar at Saragossa which had suffered greatly from the ravages of time and developed wide cracks in many places, he has an exact and unique knowledge of Goya's painting methods.

Thus at last we have available the report of an expert with long personal and practical experience of fresco-painting, who has based his findings on a close examination of the frescos *in situ* [45]. As usual we find that things are at once simpler and more complex than a casual inspection of the frescos might lead one to believe. Hitherto an exaggerated importance had been attached to the materials and procedures employed by Goya in this work; Professor Stolz's approach is on a very different and, to our mind, higher level, when he affirms that always a great painter leaves the imprint of his genius on even the most ordinary technique. Or, to put it differently, in the beginning is the word, that is to say the inspiration, the vision; the choice of tools and technical means is secondary. There is still an all too common idea (we might call it the materialistic fallacy) that because the qualities which go to make a masterpiece remain something of a mystery, these must be the result of some procedure or device whose "secret" is unknown. Nevertheless, as Stolz points out, a fresco never lies; it reveals promptly and unmistakably the way the painter went to work, as well as much about his temperament.

But, to read aright the message conveyed by a fresco as regards the artist's temperament and mode of working, we need to study it from close at hand. In the case of frescos, distance tends to blur the execution and to blend into the general effect brushstrokes that, closely studied, might have much to tell us. In the present instance it seemed *prima facie* unlikely that for no special reason the painter would have had recourse to a slower, more exacting technique than that of true fresco, which makes it possible to cover quickly and effectively large surfaces such as the San Antonio cupola. We find no niggling delicacy in Goya's fresco art, no needless lingering over minutiae of description, no trace of effort; on the contrary, what strikes us most in the San Antonio frescos is the rapidity with which they must have been painted, the breadth and verve of their execution. Goya has built up his composition in large masses flooded with light, with vigorous brushstrokes, dazzling contrasts. We have already suggested that few of Goya's works can have given him the same feeling of complete independence as did these frescos. After his disastrous physical breakdown, he had come back to life and was eager to express himself in a large-scale work. These murals were a heaven-sent opportunity; here at last he had not to fear any pressure from ecclesiastics or the censure of his colleagues. Presumably he was left to himself on his scaffolding; in any case his deafness must have discouraged visitors. His fresco technique, Stolz assures us, is flawless but, as we would expect from Goya, never uniform or monotonous. He bends it to his needs, sometimes letting his brush glide delicately over passages lightly washed with color, sometimes building up a thick impasto, giving certain passages a strong relief, by mixing sand into the paint. In a word, he outdistanced even the boldest painters of his day and ours in La Florida.

These paintings were made *a fresco* in the exact sense, though (as Stolz has noticed) Goya added retouchings in tempera here and there, especially where he wished to conceal the joins which are bound to exist, when the paint has dried, between the area covered on a given day and the following day's work. Sometimes when he needs a color effect unobtainable on damp plaster, he paints *a secco* in isolated tones. (This is the case with vermilion and blue whose drawbacks in *buon fresco* painting were well known to all readers of Palomino.) One of the things that strikes us when we examine these frescos in close-up is the curious manner in which the color has been put on in places, and what we observe confirms a statement made by his first biographers: that Goya smeared on the paint with his fingers when the fancy took him. Also, here and there, so as to lighten a tone or break up a too densely textured passage, he scratched the wet color with his nails—an expeditious but effective procedure that assuredly does not figure in any painter's manual [46].

But though we may find improvisations of this order in details of the forms Goya conjured up on the walls, it was quite otherwise with his handling of color. Here there was no question of improvising, but a test of painterly *savoir-faire*—which Goya possessed abundantly, as well as much experience in this particular field. Before he climbed up his scaffolding he carefully chose his colors. Experience had taught him in advance the exact effect produced by a wash of liquid pigment on a surface of wet lime plaster and he had to reckon with the fact that colors always are darker when the plaster is freshly laid, and as it dries tend to become much lighter, with the result that there is a marked difference between the intensity of the colors when newly applied and in their final state. In short the painter needs to know the technical procedure appropriate to his medium and to take into account the way each color will behave, its solidity and durability.

Goya—it cannot be too often repeated—expressed form in terms of light and color and this explains why he never called on line and drawing to provide a rigid framework for the painted image; only to supply rough indications of the place to be occupied by each picture element. We see this clearly in the San Antonio frescos. On close inspection it becomes evident that the lines Goya incised in the plaster were not intended to be definitive. This can be seen in photographs made at a very short distance from the wall and especially in those which were taken in a slanting light. When it came to the actual painting Goya departed widely from his initial scheme and in constructing his forms often indulged in improvisations due to the inspiration of the moment. Needless to say, he was not the first or only painter to act in this way; many Baroque artists had taken similar liberties. But in Goya's time this meant a deliberate revolt against the Mengs tradition of careful preparation and controlled execution. Mengs would never have dreamt of climbing his scaffolding and starting work until he had plotted out his composition down to the last detail, and he had imbued Francisco Bayeu with these ideas. Hence the violent quarrels between Goya and his orthodox-minded brother-in-law when he was painting the "Virgin, Queen of Martyrs" fresco in the cathedral of El Pilar at Saragossa.

What was novel—all but unique, as Stolz assures us—in Goya's handling of color in San Antonio was that he used black or the greys resulting from its admixture with the white plaster as his ground color. On this ground he conjured up effects of volume by the use of suitably contrasting, brighter tones; even when keeping to the true fresco technique, he had no qualms about employing scumbles and touches of stronger hues telling out on the ground tint (these come out clearly in our color photographs). But whether it was Goya himself or an assistant who effaced with tempera the joins or "seams" that would otherwise have been visible between portions of the wall painted on successive days, it is going too far to speak of a "mixed technique" as some have done. As for what may be called the myth of the sponges, Stolz points out that sponges are quite unsuitable for fresco-painting, and these presumably were used merely for washing the artist's palette. In short Beruete's theory is quite untenable.

The so-called retouchings—in, for instance, the angels' garments—where the separate brushstrokes are clearly marked with a view to heightening the effect, are merely rapid touches slashed with a heavily charged brush upon the ground tint. Hence the over-all impression of tremendous vitality produced by these dazzling, boldly applied streaks of color, and it is these that give their tonal values to the fabrics, lights and figures. The San Antonio frescos well may rank as a first and brilliant demonstration of what might be called "the aesthetic of effect," in which impressions are recorded with the maximum expressive vigor; an aesthetic that has steadily gained ground in painting, from Goya's time to ours. *Effect*, then, first and foremost—and the effect these artists have in mind is as Malraux says "the very style of anguish," that rankling unrest which we discern in Goya's art and which throughout the 19th century makes its presence felt, latently or overtly, in European art.

GOYA AS A MURAL PAINTER

When Goya started work at La Florida he had a long experience of decorative art and fresco-painting behind him, and a brief account seems called for here of the part played by previous undertakings of this kind in the shaping of his genius. Moreover, this will enable the reader better to understand how it was he came to produce a work so brilliantly original in conception and execution as the San Antonio frescos. The emergence of Goya in a climate seemingly so unpropitious as that of the 18th century and in the lineage of the Spanish school, then in a state of hopeless decadence as compared with what it had been a century earlier, has sometimes been regarded as something of a prodigy, intriguing and inexplicable, and his genius as wholly self-begotten.

Though bewildered by the change of taste that followed the coming of the Bourbons, Spanish 18th-century artists did their best, if a feeble best, to uphold the traditions of the 17th century, when they found Baroque being challenged by an art far less congenial to the Spanish temperament. This conflict of styles lasted all through the 18th century and made itself felt particularly in the Court painting of the age, now that the Spanish Bourbon monarchs, from Philip V to Charles III, had summoned foreign artists, French and Italian, to Madrid. The Italians stood for Baroque tradition at its purest, modified only by the addition of rococo effects of a somewhat precious, over-sophisticated order. Meanwhile French artists, specializing as they did in genre art or the classical type of portrait, brought to Spain both their taste for order and proportion and tendencies towards a colder, less adventurous form of art. As the century progressed the antagonism between these two conflicting schools of art came to a head and, under Charles III, Madrid was the scene of some sensational clashes between the champions of Baroque and those of Neo-Classicism, which latter, with the coming of the Age of Enlightenment, had been promoted to the rank of a dogma, absolute and infallible. In Madrid those two famous artists, Giovanni Battista Tiepolo and Anton Raphael Mengs, were the leaders of the conflicting movements. Both had been called in by the Spanish Court to paint the ceilings of the new Royal Palace, inaugurated by Charles III in 1764, and the juxtaposition of their frescos dramatically revealed the incompatibility of the two schools of art. Tiepolo's were not only his last work (he died in 1770) but the swan-song of Venetian painting at its noblest, and also of Baroque. Mengs, on the other hand, with his linear style, his frigid imitations of the works of pagan antiquity and his doctrine of the *beau idéal,* pointed the way that neo-classical painting was henceforth to follow in Spain.

Whether because this fell in with his natural inclinations, or out of deference to a well-established national tradition, Goya in his youth espoused the cause of Baroque art. Little as is known about his stay in Italy, we know enough to realize it played a part in the shaping of his talent. The fact that in his old age he said his only masters were Velazquez, Rembrandt and Nature need not be taken too literally or lead us to interpret his art in isolation from his more immediate past. As I have already set forth my views on the problem of Goya's artistic background[47], I confine myself here to a brief résumé.

Born in 1746, Goya showed an aptitude for art at a very early age. When only thirteen, he entered the studio of José Luzán, a rather mediocre painter practising at Saragossa. Dissatisfied with the progress he was making in this narrow, provincial environment, he made two trips to Madrid, in 1763 and 1766, to take part in competitions (with money prizes) sponsored by the Royal Academy of San Fernando. He failed on both occasions. Perhaps he was by nature unamenable to any academic discipline; in any case he seems to have been an unsatisfactory pupil and it is certain that he cherished no kindly memory of his teachers. This, I think, is what he wanted to convey when he said that his "only masters" were Velazquez, Rembrandt and Nature. The sort of teaching current in the studios and academies of the time must have irked a young artist of the type of Goya, high-spirited, eager to indulge in flights of fancy, and doubtless insubordinate. A genius never makes a good pupil. In any case a youth as passionately conscious of his vocation as Goya cannot have felt at ease in such surroundings. After a precocious start he took a long time to find himself and had much ground to cover before producing works of real merit. Nevertheless his early paintings, though completely overshadowed by the achievements of his maturity, should not be ignored; they deserve more careful study than has so far been given them, if only for the light they throw on his later development.

Goya was not one of those artists who achieve perfection at the first attempt. Given his unruly temperament and highly personal ideas on painting, he was inevitably and passionately hostile to the spirit of an age which, under the deadening influence of Neo-Classicism, was now beginning to make a cult of strict decorum and moderation in all things. Here lies the interest, historical and even ethical, of his early years of struggle and unremitting toil. Subsequently his development was speeded up by what we have called the "crises" of his life, those dramatic moments when personal predicaments (illnesses and deafness) or external factors (war, political upheavals, exile) provoked reactions so violent that he was moved to express himself with an ever greater boldness in his art.

But Goya did not seek inspiration only from within; he had a keen eye for the world around him and, like the bearded old man in the drawing he made at Bordeaux towards the close of his life, could say right up to the end "I'm still learning." And it is not only in schools that one learns. In his daily life, on his travels, and in the works of painters who interested him, he never failed to scan with keen attention anything that appealed to his insatiable curiosity or might enlarge his field of action. We need only recall that at the age of thirty-two, he took up etching (in which he subsequently made good as one of the world's great masters); that, when seventy-three, he became interested in the then new process of lithography and produced some masterpieces in that medium; and, finally, that when he was seventy-eight he turned his hand to miniature-painting on ivory.

There is no doubt that Goya's visit to Italy greatly added to his store of knowledge, for he can hardly have learnt more than the rudiments of art at Saragossa. How long he stayed in Italy is uncertain but by the time he returned to Spain, in 1771, he had made great forward strides. He had learnt, *inter alia*, fresco-painting and no sooner was he back than, with juvenile enthusiasm, he plunged into a difficult, large-scale work he was invited to undertake in his native province.

Three times in his life Goya was called on to decorate church interiors and each of these major works was a milestone in his career. These were: in 1771-1772, the decorations in the vault of the *coreto* (small choir) in the cathedral of Nuestra Señora del Pilar at Saragossa; in 1780-1781, in the dome of the same church, a fresco representing *The Virgin, Queen of Martyrs*; in 1798, the San Antonio frescos, his supreme achievement in this field. These three works are well worth studying seriatim for the light they throw on the development of Goya's genius over a period of nearly thirty years.

The best, most comprehensive survey of Goya's frescos thus far published is to be found in an article by Ramón Stolz [48]; one of its outstanding merits is the stress he lays on many points completely neglected or overlooked in previous monographs on Goya. The gist of what Professor Stolz has to say is this. When Goya returned to Saragossa from Italy in 1771, a host of impressions gathered in the course of his trip were simmering in his mind. He must still have been full of that first fine rapture which a sojourn abroad so often induces in impressionable young men. Of Saragossa's famous pair of cathedrals (La Seo is the older), that of Nuestra Señora del Pilar is remarkable in that it has two altars and two choirs. Placed in the center of the church, the high altar is decorated with a magnificent stone reredos in Spanish Renaissance style, made by the sculptor Damián Forment; just beyond this is the main choir, with three rows of stalls, reserved for the canons of the cathedral. But in the second bay behind the high altar, in a small, shrine-like recess of richly worked marble, stands an altar dedicated to the much-venerated "Virgen del Pilar" (so called after the pillar of jasper on which the Virgin is said to have alighted when she appeared to St James), and it is this altar which attracts the greater number of worshippers. In 1750 the architect Ventura Rodriguez—later a close friend of Goya, who made a portrait of him—was called in to restore the interior of the edifice and to build the chapel of El Pilar; it was consecrated in 1765. Opposite the chapel, flush with the enclosing wall of the church, is the second choir, the *coreto* [49]. It was the extremely lofty vault of this choir that Goya was asked to decorate in 1771—his first work as a frescoist.

A well-known figure in Saragossa art circles of the time, Ventura Rodriguez no doubt met Goya soon after his return from Italy, when the young painter was eager to get work and make a name for himself in his native province. Goya was given the commission in October 1771 [50] and on November 11 submitted a sample piece of fresco-painting as proof of his proficiency in this medium. His work having been duly examined and approved, on January 27, 1772 he presented a sketch of the fresco he proposed to paint and this, too, was approved of, Goya being complimented on having produced a "skillful piece of work, in very nice taste indeed" [51]. The committee even decided not to trouble about consulting the Royal Academy, as had been originally intended. Goya signed the contract on January 28, 1772, and on the 31st received an advance of 5,000 reals, on account of the 15,000 promised him for the work. A document dated July 31, 1772, informs us that the balance was paid to Goya on that date; as a matter of fact the work had been finished as early as June 1. Assuming he began on February 1, as seems probable, it took him exactly four months to paint some sixty square yards of wall surface.

There are, I think, two main reasons why critics have devoted little attention to these frescos; for one thing, they are difficult to see, being at a considerable height above floor level, and, secondly, no really good photographs of them exist. They were studied in detail for the first time by Ramón Stolz when he restored them several years ago and he was also the first to realize the significance of this youthful work, so full of promise for the future. The subject set was of a kind well suited to the Baroque style at its most effusive: *The Adoration of the Name of God.* Keeping closely to tradition, Goya peopled an undulating cloud-bank with a choir of angels forming a sweeping curve around the triangle symbolizing the Trinity, which tells out to wonderful effect above the billowing clouds that fill the upper part of the composition. Both sketch and finished work had hitherto been dismissed out of hand, as being devoid of originality, for the good reason that the fresco itself had never been carefully examined under favorable conditions. Actually the subject here is the same as that—treated somewhat differently, it is true—which we find in the apse of San Antonio de la Florida. Stolz regards this fresco as doubly interesting. On the one hand, "it has very great psychological value" as an illustration of Goya's characteristic brio, the irrepressible zest with which, at the age of twenty-six, he flung himself into the work. And, secondly, it reveals his gifts at an early stage of his career, and "on a greatly magnified scale, as if an enlarging mirror were held up to them, the gropings, uncertainties and misgivings of young genius at odds with itself and with the spirit of the age."

Here his gifts as a colorist are already well in evidence, though the execution still shows a lack of self-confidence and his palette has not the rich variety and brilliance it was later to acquire. Even so, some of the characteristics of his style, notably his fondness for technical shortcuts, are making their appearance. All is bathed in golden light and the whole fresco has that warm tonality, dear to Baroque painters, which we find at its best in the art of Luca Giordano. Even in this early work Goya was beginning to expel from his palette the dark colors so lavishly employed by his predecessors: in particular raw sienna and the "antique umber" *(ombra antigua)* spoken of by Palomino.

Even in the Baroque composition and over-all tonality of this fresco there are striking anticipations of the style which nowadays is called "Goyesque." Particularly interesting, as forerunners of the figures in La Florida, are the angels clad in flowing drapery and wearing those curiously unconvincing wings which we find so often in Goya's later depictions of angelic beings. There is no question that this work is imbued with the spirit of Italian art in general, not only Italian Baroque. The angels on the left, as Stolz has justly noticed, remind us (especially in the treatment of the heads) of the technique of Roman classical painting. In this early fresco Goya obviously owed much to what he had seen of both Baroque art and classical antiquity and found in these a pretext for some of his first innovations; for example, the technique which Stolz describes as "divisionist," the use of parallel streaks of reds, greys and greens merging optically at a distance—a technique he was to employ twenty-seven years later at San Antonio, with uncompromising boldness. When he examined the *coreto* fresco in close-up, Stolz was struck by other anticipations of the fresco in the cupola. "Here Goya's nerves were strung up to the breaking-point; with twitching hands, he dug his nails into the colored plaster, tearing great rents in it that revealed the dazzling white of the intonaco." Such is the broadness and vigor of the execution that, even when seen at a considerable distance, this fresco still looks like a much enlarged preliminary sketch. Characteristic of Goya's style, this sketch-like technique (which so much disgusted Bayeu some years later) stemmed directly from his synthetic vision of reality.

Stolz goes so far as to detect "in the small, roughly blocked-in groups in the distance (visible only on a close-up view) the hand of the prodigious etcher and draftsman responsible for *The Caprices, The Disasters of War* and so many drawings built up in a sort of creative frenzy with masses of darks and lights." Thus, though the *coreto* paintings are the work of "a virgin talent" and a painter of little technical experience, Goya, as far back as 1771, had already started on the path he was destined so triumphantly to follow.

It seems possible that, in addition to these Italian reminiscences, Goya was influenced, more directly, by the fresco made several years earlier in this same church by the Madrilenian painter Antonio González Velázquez. Youngest of a family of artists, painters and sculptors, Antonio, like Goya, had just come back from Italy when he began his decorations in El Pilar. He was twenty-two years old and had been studying in Rome with Corrado Giaquinto. Stolz, who has a high opinion of this work by González Velázquez, is convinced that its freshness of inspiration and flexible technique must have made a far deeper impression on Goya than did later the stiff and formal paintings of his brother-in-law Francisco Bayeu, from his earliest days a fervent devotee of Mengs. Some years later Goya struck up a friendship with González Velázquez, with whom he had so much in common, and in 1781, when Bayeu was making trouble over his paintings in the dome of El Pilar, it was this young, forward-looking artist whom he invited to arbitrate between them.

The frescos in the Carthusian monastery of Aula Dei near Saragossa were painted in 1772-1774 or thereabouts, according to information given by Father Tomás López in the notes he supplied to Carderera. These paintings have been even less studied and less often reproduced than those in the *coreto* of El Pilar. They were already in extremely poor condition at the beginning of the present century and, worse still, part of the work was repainted by two French artists, Amédée and Paul Buffet, who actually signed them! Beruete managed to get some tolerable photographs which he published in his book. These paintings form a sort of frieze some sixteen feet above the floor level of the church and, no scaffolding being available, it has been impossible for us to study them in detail. Beruete thinks they were painted in oils. Distinctive are their reddish color-scheme, their obvious Italianism and the sobriety of the composition in vertical lines. Few in number, boldly designed and built up in well-marked planes, the figures have a monumental quality. This is largely due to the conditions of their presentation, in a frieze, but also to their great size and the fewness of gestures. Here there are definite recalls of Tiepolo; doubtless Goya had seen and studied the frescos recently painted by the great Venetian in the new Royal Palace of Madrid.

Between the *coreto* frescos and Goya's next venture in this field eight years intervened; eight crowded years of intensive work and constant efforts to perfect his art. It was in 1774, after his marriage to Josefa Bayeu, that he started painting cartoons for the royal tapestry factory of Santa Barbara. His first cartoons, made under the inquisitorial eye of Bayeu, were relatively unenterprising and some time had to elapse before he dared to put himself into these works. Indeed the series made in 1775 when his style was cramped by constant supervision has only recently been ascribed to him, as a result of the publication of records hitherto unavailable. Until then no one could imagine that these cartoons were by Goya's hand, so little worthy of him do they seem for the most part. But he was not a man to endure such controls for long. From 1776 on, the cartoons became more personal, his palette warmer and more varied. How rapid was this progress towards freedom can be seen if we compare his *Picnic on the Grass* of 1776 with that little masterpiece, *The Sunshade*, painted in 1777, or that delightful composition, *The Crockery Seller*, of a year later. These three years were decisive in Goya's development as a colorist; and the climax came in 1780 when he delivered a batch of eleven cartoons—amongst them *The Washerwomen*, *The Tobacco Guard* and *The Woodcutters*—in which we see his handling of color at its finest. The time had now come for Goya to take steps to consolidate his reputation and this he did—but it was not all plain sailing. To begin with, he had to get elected to the Royal Academy of San Fernando and in this at least he was successful. I must confess to not thinking much of the qualifying work presented by him, the *Crucifixion* now in the Prado; it is excessively conventional.

Though Goya's star was rising rapidly he still was far from having reached the exalted position of Francisco Bayeu, righthand man of that dictator of the arts at Madrid, the "divine" Mengs. While Goya was busy solving the compositional problems set by the cartoons, Bayeu, acclaimed by all, was painting two vaults in the cathedral of El Pilar. Bayeu was treated with much deference by the cathedral authorities who saw in him a Court Painter who had condescended to abandon for the moment his official duties in the capital as coadjutor of Mengs, so as to do honor to El Pilar with his brush. There were other vaults to be decorated and Bayeu, who had many obligations at Madrid, suggested that the work should be carried out, under his supervision, by his brother Ramón, an indifferent painter, and his brother-in-law, Goya. This was not particularly flattering for the latter, considering he had been regarded as fully competent when much younger, on his return from Italy, to paint the vault of the *coreto* of El Pilar without aid or supervision. Bayeu's proposal was approved in 1780 and in October of that year Goya and Ramón Bayeu went to Saragossa to submit preliminary sketches to the authorities. The uncertainties we sense in the early frescos were at an end; Goya had now achieved complete mastery of his means and he set to work with his usual impetuosity. The sketches were a complete success, but Goya evidently neglected to do what is expected of the conscientious frescoist and prepared no full-size cartoons. In short he trusted to the inspiration of the moment when he came to the actual painting. Francisco Bayeu was thoroughly shocked by such proceedings, and made no secret of his disapproval.

There were 250 square yards of wall surface to cover, in the dome and on the pendentives. Goya worked quickly, too quickly for the liking of Bayeu who went so far as to accuse him of scamping his work—which naturally enraged him. La Viñaza published a description of the incident as recorded by Father Tomás López, a contemporary of Goya [52]. Father López says that Goya, though they were kinsmen by marriage, "could not get on with Bayeu because their views on art were so different and also because both were irritable men." Bayeu was dissatisfied with the work done in the dome "because, in his opinion, Goya had painted it much too hastily, completing the entire work in forty days. There was a stormy scene between them on the scaffolding and when Goya asked him to go down and judge of the effect seen from below, Bayeu pointed to a poor man begging in the church and bade him notice the picturesque effect of his ragged figure, viewed from above. If, he added, the beggar looked equally well whether seen from a distance or close by, it could and should be the same thing with his painting." Bayeu called on the cathedral Chapter to intervene and, when told to "correct" his work, Goya flew into a rage and talked of going back to Madrid. Next, the committee in charge of the works being carried out in the cathedral asked him to make alterations in the dome and also improvements in the preliminary studies for the pendentives "which," they said, "have not yet been finished." (This shows how little Goya's sketch-like style was understood by his contemporaries.) Things came to a head when Goya sent in a written reply, pointing out that he was under no obligation to submit his work to his brother-in-law, for his approval or otherwise, and that he would never have accepted this commission had he expected to be treated "as a mere underling and paid employee." Not until Goya's friend Father Salcedo, a Carthusian monk at Aula Dei, had intervened did Goya calm down and agree to make new sketches. The incident was closed, but it still rankled in his mind. In a letter written some years later to his friend Zapater we read: "At the mere thought of Saragossa and those paintings, my blood boils." Anyhow Goya did no more frescos at El Pilar; it was Ramón Bayeu who was given the order for the other dome. And the estrangement between the brothers-in-law lasted for several years.

If we have described these incidents at some length, this is because they throw much light on the incompatibility between Goya's painting and the type of art appreciated by his age, of which Bayeu was a notable exponent. Moreover they help us to understand his very special approach to fresco-painting and its technique. The painting in the dome which was the beginning of all the trouble, aesthetic and domestic, represented *The Virgin, Queen of Martyrs*. On the four pendentives were depicted the four cardinal virtues: Faith, Courage, Charity and Patience (the last two were sorely tried, as we have seen, on this occasion). The dome was treated in the usual Baroque style, with a ring of clouds upon which stood the martyrs encircling the Virgin, who was placed on a higher plane, dominating the entire composition, and surrounded by the angelic hosts. Bayeu began by telling Goya to alter the lay-out of the group presided over by the Virgin; this is what Goya in his letter refers to as "the main façade." As always is the case with Goya, the execution is superb. No less delightful are the colors and the brushwork of the sketches, now in the Museo Capitular of Saragossa [53]. Goya made changes when he came to the final painting in order to increase the number of angels attending the Virgin. The chief interest of the fresco in the dome lies in the renderings of some of the martyrs. The two female saints in the foreground wear dresses with close-fitting bodices, skirts and over-skirts consisting of broad bands of material[54]; Goya dressed his angels in La Florida in much the same way, but with a greater variety of decorative effects. The figure of St Paul foreshadows the man we have called, in La Florida, the "Old Testament Prophet." This shows how Goya kept to certain types of figure, though in the execution there were often drastic changes. Most of the El Pilar angels, for example the one in light colors displaying her shapely legs as she wings her way aloft, keep fairly close to Baroque tradition. As for the allegorical figures on the pendentives, that of Faith, with her sweeping gesture, the face wrapped in a white veil, and the hand carrying a chalice, is not only of great beauty but unique in the decorative painting of the epoch. Also, the cherubs with tiny wings, while obviously deriving from Tiepolo's, anticipate those in La Florida.

Goya turned to account what he had learnt in making tapestry cartoons and handled color with more freedom and finesse than in the 1772 frescos. The prevailing reddish tonality of the latter now gave place to a much lighter palette, whose effect is enhanced by the delicacy of the execution and the use of pearly hues, the whole, as Stolz points out, producing the effect of an enormous watercolor. Goya had by this time fully mastered fresco technique, and the brushwork is as spontaneous as it is original. Here and there he falls back on the white of the plaster (as the aquarellist uses the white of the paper), treating it as if it were a supplementary color. In some places the impasto is so thick as to give the impression of a miniature bas-relief[55]. Yet we feel that Goya was holding himself in and trying once again, as in the *Crucifixion*, to attune his style to the aesthetic of the day; he was all too well aware that Bayeu was there, watching him from the corner of an eye. Nevertheless his natural exuberance was always tending to break through and even where he curbed it the results found no favor with his brother-in-law. Today Bayeu's frescos in El Pilar, carefully thought out and planned down to the least detail, strike us as frigid, dull and wholly uninspired when compared with Goya's dazzling creations. True, the latter had not yet quite found himself, but already there were clear indications of his genius. As Stolz tells us, he was no longer the young, inexperienced painter of the *coreto*; his fresco technique was far in advance of that of any of his contemporaries and he was well on the way to that masterwork, the frescos in San Antonio de la Florida.

There was an interval of seventeen years between the paintings in the dome of El Pilar and the San Antonio frescos; eventful years in Goya's personal life and fruitful in the shaping of his genius. During this period he had discovered new fields of action; to begin with, from 1783 on, that of portrait-painting. How important to his art was this new development can be seen when we examine his handling of figures in, for example, *San Bernardino preaching in the Presence of King Alfonso V*, painted for the church of San Francisco el Grande, Madrid (inaugurated in 1784). Upstanding in the midst of a conventional group of personages whose piety is expressed by that "doglike gaze" of dumb devotion to which reference has been made in our account of the miracle scene, is the massive figure of the Sienese saint, whose expression is very different: imperious, full of energy. But the great merit of this work lies in the charm of the color-scheme from which all dark hues have been expelled and which resembles that employed in the El Pilar dome, allowing for the differences between fresco and oil painting.

But the devotional pictures—and this applies no less to *San Bernardino* than to those he made in 1787 for the church of Santa Ana at Valladolid, exquisite as are the delicacy and finish of the latter—cannot bear comparison with the frescos. They do little more than illustrate the conflict between two tendencies: the suavity and concern for perfect craftsmanship conspicuous in Santa Ana and the almost brutal forcefulness of the two scenes of the life of St Francis Borgia painted the following year for a chapel in Valencia Cathedral.

From 1785 on, we find a rapid improvement in Goya's technique, due to the exigencies of portrait-painting; his handling of color notably became much subtler, a tendency that culminated in his "pearl-grey period" (ca. 1790). The *Portrait of Francisco Bayeu* in grey (Prado) and the portraits of the actress La Tirana—that in the Academy of San Fernando was made about 1794—illustrate this phase. And these discoveries in the field of color were turned to wonderful account in the La Florida frescos. The ground of greyish tones on the walls of the church makes a perfect foil to the golden ochres, pale pinks and exquisite greens, dappled with touches of bright yellow, blue and red, which in turn give its full value to the ground of darker hues.

In the field of mural decoration the nearest antecedents (though there is some doubt about their date) are, to begin with, the four medallions Goya made for the library of Godoy's palace; three of them are in the Prado, the fourth has disintegrated. They are allegories of Agriculture, Industry and Commerce and their symbolism is such as one would expect of an artist so independent-minded: simple and forthright. The breadth with which the various themes are treated, the lightness and freshness of the execution, and the grey-blue tonality cannot fail to bring to mind the La Florida frescos and, assuming that they are correctly dated 1797, the similarities between the two works are easily accounted for.

There is more boldness, a richer inspiration, in the three pictures in Santa Cueva at Cadiz, an oratory founded by Don José Saez de Santa Maria, Marquis of Valdeíñigo. This is not the place to discuss these pictures in detail or to study the moot question of their exact date, which falls somewhere between 1792 and 1796. Anyhow the exact year of their making is of minor importance so far as their kinship with the La Florida frescos is concerned. That kinship is apparent in the expressionist interpretation and distortions of the human figure. This procedure, so often followed by Goya in his religious painting, need not lead us to infer that his intention was ironical or that his faith was wavering. The explanation lies, I think, elsewhere. In these works he was deliberately and violently breaking with the traditions of the heroic, idealistic religious art which now was dying out in Europe along with the Baroque style. Goya made no attempt either to glorify his figures or to invest them with the glamour of an ideal beauty in accordance with the tradition of the age into which he had been born. Nor did he let himself be hypnotized by the model; it was he and he alone who imposed his personality on the picture. Hence the obvious affinities between apostles and angels in his paintings. (We find the same thing taking place even in his depictions of Christ.) Since he has not the least wish either to render his model faithfully or to beautify it, and since, moreover, he views the theme, however sacred, from a purely matter-of-fact angle, he tends to "popularize" it or else indulges in distortion. This can be seen in the Toledo *Prendimiento* (or *Betrayal of Christ*), the Cadiz pictures and the San Antonio frescos. Nevertheless, in large-scale compositions—in, that is to say, his murals—we find a depth of feeling and an expressive power that has something in common with genuine religious emotion. This can be seen in the paintings in the church of Santa Cueva. Here Goya tackled the problems of forms presented in strong relief, of chiaroscuro and crowd scenes and solved them with his characteristically abridged technique, by means of light and volumes. These big works gave him opportunities of employing that "theatrical lighting" of which we have already spoken and thanks to which these forms acquire a dramatic instancy lifting them above the merely mundane.

In the only study of the Cadiz paintings[56] that has so far appeared César Peman rightly stresses their resemblances to the La Florida frescos. Referring to the picture of *The Miracle of the Loaves and Fishes*, he writes: "In the handling of this scene we seem to detect the touches of irony and caricature in which Goya so often indulges. Gestures and attitudes are strongly emphasized. Many of them, though frequent in his work, were clearly not taken direct from nature. Indeed we feel that between Goya's observation of his models and the moment of starting on the picture, there was an interval in which he made analytic studies of attitudes and gestures that had caught his eye, and this explains the origin of some of those figures, so strongly expressive and at the same time individualized, which we find throughout his work. Similarly, in the San Antonio miracle scene Goya may well have realized his inability to depict the miracle with the devout simplicity of the true believer, and for this reason have preferred to treat it on narrative, anecdotal lines and to stress the atmosphere of the scene rather than its religious significance."

Actually the anecdotal element in both the Santa Cueva and the San Antonio paintings is relatively slight. It would be truer to say that Goya employed no more of the iconographical data than were absolutely necessary. Apart from any question of Goya's religious convictions, his approach to his subjects is of much interest. Were it not for the halo round St Anthony's head (obviously intended to indicate his sainthood), this scene might have simply been entitled: "A monk administering last consolation to a dying beggar." Goya is, one would say, in haste to have done with the story-telling element; after indicating the halo with a few brushstrokes and grouping his figures round the saint, he promptly embarks on his real subject, that is to say painting pure and simple. When he gave free rein to his impetuous brushwork, rendering faces with a few hasty, chopped-off strokes, seemingly irrelevant, and in a sort of shorthand of his own invention, he knew very well what he was doing. As he told his brother-in-law on the scaffolding at El Pilar, all would fall into place and become intelligible when seen from below. What supremely interested him was the arrangement of the separate patches of white, greys and various shades of ochre, which were to define, interpret and bring to life the forms that, posted on his scaffolding, he conjured up in his mind's eye. That was his true vocation, and he knew it. For his preliminary sketches were mere notes, briefly jotted down, both for the paintings in La Florida and for those in Santa Cueva where, moreover, his approach was on very similar lines. In *The Last Supper*, for instance, the apostles who are lying on the ground in a circle around Christ as they take their frugal meal, might well be tramps who are sheltering from a storm or resting after trudging the roads all day. Their faces are uncouth, have little spirituality, and even in Christ's figure we find nothing of beauty or benignity. Indeed here, again, it is only the conventional halo and the central place He occupies in the composition that make known his more-than-human status. Nevertheless, the lighting, the atmosphere of hushed suspense, the utter weariness we sense in the recumbent bodies and the awareness of impending tragedy perceptible on these peasant faces—all make us feel that Goya here was gripped by some profound emotion, transcending the purely iconographical frame of reference, expressible in terms of painting and of painting only.

Something similar, this feeling of the tragic sense of life, though expressed differently, can be detected in the faces of *The Caprices*, still more dramatically in those of *The Disasters of War*, and finally, transposed into the realm of the fantastic, in the weird monsters of the *Disparates*. Born into an age of storm and stress, Goya lost no opportunity of expressing his tragic vision of the human predicament, though he ranged in quest of his materials far beyond the confines of traditional religious art. Carried away by his enthusiasm for Goya, André Villebœuf went so far as to describe Santa Cueva as "one of the greatest revelations in the whole world's painting" [57]. What is so remarkable in the composition of the Santa Cueva paintings—what indeed holds them together—is not merely the over-all effect of the lighting, admirably controlled and integrated though it be, but also that of the masses of figures brought to vivid life by the magic of Goya's brush. It is to the crowd of agitated figures in the background of *The Miracle of the Loaves and Fishes* that the scene owes its dramatic, all-pervading vibrancy.

San Antonio gave him a wider field of action and subjects better suited to the bold, untrammelled brushwork that came naturally to him. Also he probably saw in it a heaven-sent opportunity for painting without any need to trouble about the opinion of others and to create, rapidly and fancy-free, one of his masterpieces—or anyhow the work that, as things turned out, was to mark the climax of his career as a fresco-painter.

For Goya was destined never to get another commission for work of this order. But once again he had to face a nerve-shattering experience whose effect was both to intensify his feelings of revolt against life's ignominies and to incite him to take even greater liberties in his art. Those six terrible years of the War of Independence (1808-1814), years of turmoil, peril and horror, left their imprint both on his personality and his work, and at the same time heightened yet more his powers of expression. His pessimistic view of humanity comes out to the full in *The Disasters of War*. Yet even the savagery of the war years and their aftermath counted less for him than his utter disillusionment. This disillusionment of a man whose life had had so many vicissitudes and who had witnessed so many catastrophes found expression in grotesque visions of unbelievable and futile monsters, those of the *Disparates* (or *Proverbs*) and the "black paintings" of the Deaf Man's House.

From the documentary evidence now available [58] the latter appear to have been made in 1819-1820. Coming twenty years after the La Florida frescos, these "black paintings" prove that in his old age Goya had lost nothing of his interest in, and aptitude for, mural painting. Looking at the bare walls of his country house, he was seized with a desire to clothe them with the phantasmagoria of his dreams. And instead of continuing his etchings, he took up his brush again. The expressionist drive behind his painting and his technique made itself more apparent than ever before in the murals of the Quinta del Sordo. Like many other great painters, he felt most at ease when dealing with a large-scale work giving full scope to his creative inspiration. Yet, allowing for the differences between a royal commission for the decoration of a church and the macabre, unrestrained fantasy that gave birth to the "black paintings," we can discern many points in common between the two works.

What we find in the Quinta del Sordo murals is a sort of glorification of the same procedures, but here employed in darkly terrifying visions of witches' sabbaths, of brutality and the mythology of death. As in his etchings, Goya makes much use of black-and-white effects on a grey monochrome in which earth colors only are employed, and creates the illusion of color with light after-touches. On the walls of his home Goya the Saturnian depicted the phantoms of his solitude and rankling unrest. Black humor and black painting. But despite the limited range of color, there is the same well-nigh reckless violence as in the San Antonio frescos, the same expressive power behind these massive forms, charged with sinister significance, arising from a dark background splashed at random on the walls. At the bidding of Goya's brush these figures come to life, the eerie, hallucinative life their creator willed for them, far other than the life imparted by "painters of reality."

The heads, rendered with a few slashes of the brush, of San Antonio are next of kin to those in the Deaf Man's House. But in the latter the "Dostoevsky type" we have spoken of in an earlier chapter is brought forward from the middle ground to the foreground. To the same family of figures belong the witches, the phlegmatic, vacant-eyed pilgrims, the two men battering each other's heads with cudgels, and the hideous picture of Saturn devouring one of his children—all the cruel, monstrous figures of the "black paintings." The open sunlit platform on which the witnesses of the miracle were standing has here become a gloomy cavern through which we have glimpses of hell. Here all the specters of Goya's private inferno have been let loose, spawn of the imagination of a man who has cut himself off from a world that, though it lavished favors on him, had nothing better to offer than an endless spectacle of human stupidity and cruelty.

GOYA'S RETURN TO LA FLORIDA

The little church of La Florida owes its celebrity to Goya's frescos. All admirers of his work, Spaniards and foreigners alike, make a point of visiting it; and we hope this book may help to a better understanding and enjoyment of what they see there. The great painter's remains, as well as one of his finest works, are housed in this humble edifice, which serves exclusively as a shrine for ever dedicated to his memory, now that Mass is celebrated there only once a year, on each anniversary of his death. When, posted on his scaffolding, Goya was painting the walls of San Antonio, he can have little thought that he was decorating his "pantheon." But many long years were to pass before he was given this last resting-place; eventful years in which his prestige gradually ripened. And as if to add a typically Goyesque touch to his return to the bank of the little river Manzanares which he had so greatly loved, a weirdly macabre incident, described on a later page, took place at the exhumation of the artist's body.

Perhaps the cruelest affliction of old age is disillusionment, and Goya tasted this to the full. When the War of Independence ended in 1814 he soon saw that there could be no question of putting the clock back; the good times were ended for him. Old and with no social ties, he realized that Madrid was no longer a place for him or for his art. Ferdinand VII, the new king, was a reactionary of the deepest dye, hostile to even the mildest form of liberalism, and Goya must have been completely out of sympathy with his royal patron. Most of the men he had known and liked were in prison or in exile; some of them accused of being *afrancesados* ("collaborators" as we would call them today), others of being progressives. In 1820 a strong liberal movement got under way, causing—since Spain is *par excellence* a land of extremists—new outbursts of violence and disorder in many parts of the country. We may assume that Goya was in sympathy with this movement, which—yet another disillusion!—came to an untimely end, with the invasion of Spain by a French army. And when in 1823, as a result, Ferdinand was solidly re-instated on the throne, he embarked on a policy of stern reprisals. In 1824, feeling more than ever out of his element in Madrid or perhaps because of the new family tie he had created, Goya applied for leave to take the waters at Plombières in France. Did he really intend to go there or was this merely a pretext to get out of Spain? Anyhow, at the age of seventy-eight he started forth on this journey, far from an easy one in those days. During a brief stay at Bordeaux he met several old friends, liberal émigrés: Goicoechea, Moratín and Silvela; then he went on to Paris. On his return to Bordeaux (September 1824) he set up house with that domineering lady Doña Leocadia Zorrilla [59], who very soon had the old man under her thumb. He revisited Madrid in 1826, to apply for sanction to renew his leave *sine die*. Ferdinand received him graciously and granted his request, imposing only one condition, that he should sit to Vicente López for his portrait.

Meanwhile there was no sign of any flagging of his inspiration either in painting or in the new art of lithography. As in the past his indomitable creative energy had enabled him to overcome the handicap of isolation from the outside world, so now his amazing vitality enabled him to overcome the serious illnesses of this last phase of his life. He died on April 16, 1828, and was buried in the family vault of his friends the Muguiros, beside his son's father-in-law, Don Martín Miguel de Goicoechea [60].

Goya's remains were destined to lie for many years in France in the cemetery of the Grande Chartreuse at Bordeaux. The times had changed, and with them the fashions of the day. But, as long as he lived, Goya's art was fated never to fall in line with them; neither in 1775 when Mengs' style was everywhere triumphant, nor in 1820 when David's followers preached to willing ears the doctrines of Neo-Classicism and Don Vicente López was the official portrait-painter of the Spanish court. Nor in the period following Goya's death did any artists follow up the paths he had explored; and meanwhile the troubled state of Spain under Isabella II told against a better understanding of his work in his own country.

Nevertheless throughout the 19th century his reputation rose steadily and a sort of legend gathered round his personality. His etchings had already, even in his lifetime, won the admiration of the most enlightened spirits of the age. Subsequently some men of discernment, few but eminent—Delacroix, Victor Hugo and Baudelaire—sensed the significance of Goya's art for the future. And occasionally, in some badly documented books of the first half of the 19th century, we have glimpses of a vague interest in his art [61]. However, since nearly all his paintings were only to be seen in Spain, he was far from having that international renown which today is at its height; not only abroad but in his own country his technical innovations met with no response for nearly half a century. After all, this is not surprising; not until, during the last thirty years of the 19th century, there developed a new way of seeing, a new attitude to art, could his message be accepted in its entirety.

In 1863, thirty-five years after Goya's death, the Royal Academy of San Fernando published for the first time *The Disasters of War*, and a year later the *Disparates* (or *Proverbs*); so far only a few isolated proofs had been in circulation and these had remained in the hands of connoisseurs. The publication of the entire series of etchings revealed some of the salient characteristics of Goya's art, the climax of certain tendencies of which signs had been apparent in *The Caprices*. Thereafter Spanish and French writers began to publish more or less fully documented studies of the artist's life and work; in short, Goya's "resurrection" was under way. The Impressionists admired and studied him and he was hailed as a precursor of the new painting that was coming to birth.

As regards the San Antonio paintings the year 1878 is of some significance since it was then that an excellent Spanish engraver, José María Galván, made copper-plates of all the San Antonio frescos—an early indication of the growing interest in this work [62].

A long-delayed act of homage to Goya remained to be fulfilled, that of transferring his remains to his native land. The Spanish Ambassador in Paris in 1888 was Don Manuel Silvela, son of one of Goya's friends who moved to Bordeaux at the same time as he, and Don Joaquín Pereyra, Spanish consul at Bordeaux, was instructed to get permission from the local authorities for the transfer. The Royal Academy of San Fernando petitioned the Spanish government to arrange for the conveyance of the body to Spain. On November 16, 1888, when the tomb in the Bordeaux cemetery was opened, the coffins of Goya and Goicoechea were found side by side and there was no means of distinguishing between them. And—as if to add a final touch of gruesomeness, the atmosphere of a *caprice fantastique*—it was discovered that the body which seemed more likely to be Goya's had no head! When and why this act of sacrilege was committed remains a mystery, all the greater since there were no signs of the coffins' having been tampered with. And—crowning irony—a ministerial crisis having arisen at Madrid, the two bodies had to be re-interred. Many years went by, years of deep anxiety in the life of Spain, before steps were taken to repatriate the remains of one of her greatest artists. The problem of identification was solved, after a fashion, by deciding to bring back *both* bodies and bury them together. On June 6, 1899[63], the coffin reached Madrid, but Goya's remains were not interred until May 11, 1900, when they were placed in a mausoleum constructed by the Spanish government in the cemetery of San Isidro.

By this time San Antonio had become a place of pilgrimage for artists and art historians. When in 1881 it was converted into a parish church, services were held in it more frequently. Under these conditions there was obviously the risk that damage might be done to the frescos by the smoke of tapers burning just below them and the fumes of incense; also there was the danger of fire now that the church was in constant use. Accordingly the Academy of San Fernando took action, and their first step was to get the church classified as an "historic building." Next they sent a report to the authorities concerned, pointing out the dangers to which the cupola and its art treasures were exposed. It was suggested that another parish church identical in aspect should be erected in the vicinity and the proposal was favorably received. However, several years passed before the site was acquired and the new church built, under the supervision of Don Juan Moya.

Meanwhile it had been decided to inter the remains of Goya in the church he had done so much to glorify; the ceremony took place at San Antonio de la Florida on November 29, 1919. Finally, in 1928, the hundredth anniversary of the artist's death, the step the Academy had been advocating for many years was taken[64]; daily services were no longer held in the old church, of which the Academy now took charge. Nevertheless it still belonged, in principle, to the Royal Patrimony, until on April 21, 1928, King Alfonso XIII formally made it over to the Royal Academy of San Fernando which from that date has spared no pains in keeping it intact, and whose duty and pride it is to safeguard the mortal remains and one of the masterworks of our great painter.

EPILOGUE

UNDER the cupola of La Florida Goya sleeps his final sleep, a sleep at last untroubled by bad dreams. Even in the grave he was to be the victim of some ghoulish creature who might have stepped out of *The Disasters of War* or the *Disparates*: the man who mutilated his dead body. But, could he have foreseen this, it would hardly have surprised him. He knew of what foulnesses man is capable and had expressed it time and again in those drawings and etchings where he lays bare the human soul.

So here he lies at rest, but not alone; above him, massed in the cupola, is a muster of the personages he had conjured up with the magic of his brush, envoys from the land of specters. There we have Goya's world in its entirety, indeed one might almost say it is his all too lucid vision of mankind that keeps watch over Goya's tomb.

For the fresco in the cupola is not only a prodigious feat of craftsmanship but a résumé of Goya's art. Faithful to the aesthetic and even to the ethic of his country and his day, he saw in Man the artist's proper study. And if we realize exactly what Man meant to him, we are well on the way to grasping the true nature of his genius, that is to say understanding both his conception of life and the meaning of the pictorial language he employed. Goya discerned in Man an infinite capacity for folly or caprice; his art is one long, impassioned study of the vagaries and vicissitudes of the human situation. Man is at once the victim of his fate and its collaborator; Goya is far from seeing him with the simplicity of the medieval eye, as having easy access to the celestial plane and comforted by a sense of the fatherly nearness of his Creator. Nor could he accept the flattering solutions of the humanists who placed man on a pedestal, an heroic figure worthy to stand beside the gods. Also, in his appraisal of man as he really is Goya did not hesitate to discard all the rhetorical devices of Baroque which, in the last analysis, were little more than pale reflections of the humanist ideal. For in the course of the centuries that had elapsed between the Middle Ages and Goya's time, European man had gradually lost his simple, unquestioning faith and acquiescence in his destiny as willed by God; he had lost, too, those illusions of his power and greatness which had meant so much to him in the golden age of the Renaissance, and even the capacity for that realistic approach to the facts of life which had found expression in Baroque art. Even that faith in the saving grace of Reason which in the earlier part of the 18th century had meant so much to the western world had been rudely shattered by the grim realities of bloodthirsty revolutions, invasions, pillage and rapine—blind, insensate stirrings of the beast within. And it was from the debris of Reason that there arose the monsters which haunted Goya's dreams.

They made their first appearance in *The Caprices*, whose lesson is that man is a slave of his passions, a helpless puppet in the hands of destiny. His brief glimmerings of rationality serve only to make him feel more acutely the burden of his responsibility and his utter degradation. But, viewed as a tragi-comedy, the innumerable aspects and antics of that pathetic creature, man, can be of enthralling interest. Goya knew this and all his work testifies to his passion for re-creating the eccentricities of human conduct.

Without exaggeration we may say it is the human theme which gives their supreme value to the frescos of La Florida; the value not only of a work of art, but also of a testimony. For around the painted railing are assembled all the type-figures of Goya's world. One might almost say that the most colorful personages of *The Caprices*, *The Disasters of War* and the *Disparates* have been invited to participate in this reunion. But, after we have taken a last look at these figures, what lingers in the memory is not so much their physical appearance as their human significance.

The pretext for bringing together all these persons—men and women, young and old, and even children—was the miracle. However it was not the miracle itself that interested Goya but the representation of the onlookers and bystanders. Characters and passions, impulses and penchants, all are recorded with superlative technical skill in the faces that look down, as from a balcony, upon the place where their maker lies at rest. Here we have eager youth, still capable of idealism ("the ecstatic"), or calm and pensive ("the non-participant"), or impressionable ("the emotive" in the Russian smock); and shy timidity ("the man with the doglike gaze" who is clasping in his arms the resuscitated corpse). The "Old Testament Prophet" is the typical seeker after righteousness, the man with a "message"; the "superstitious man" might symbolize the weakling, easily alarmed but hoping vaguely for the best; while the "proud man" in green with a big ruff is one of those complacent persons who preen themselves on their blue blood. As for the saint himself, he is not so much the miracle-worker one would expect as a man completely wrapped up in the duties of his calling; hence his conscientious, circumspect, almost professional air.

The "toothless beggar" is envy and malice personified, while "the blind man with the staff" is a symbol of decrepit old age. Noteworthy, too, are the ox-like indifference of the African Negro, the furtive, almost bestial curiosity of the "moujik" and the cringing pusillanimity of "the man with the hawk nose." Most of the males in this cross-section of the race, it will be noticed, belong to the poorest class. Like Solana and Picasso, Goya is obviously fascinated by the variety of ways in which poverty can stigmatize a face. For its outward effects are far from uniform; the hardships and humiliations it inflicts seem to bring out the essential structure of its victims, faces and bodies alike, with ruthless clarity; it is as though even on the lowest rung of the ladder, the outcast makes a despairing effort to retain the one thing he can call his own: his personality. Here poverty and misery are, in fact, the common measure of most of the male figures. Distress is what we read on the face of the man recalled to life, when for a brief moment the veil of death is lifted and he looks out on the world of day with startled eyes. We read it even in the bold, blasé gaze of the half-famished vagabond; on the pallid faces of the poor folk bearded like apostles and on the faces of many of the "non-participants." Some are pathetic-looking beggars whimpering appeals for charity; but there are more aggressive types, whose mouths are twisted in an ugly leer—for example "the man with the gorilla's head" and his companion, both of them next of kin, in character and looks alike, to the weird beings on the walls of the Deaf Man's House. These secondary personages form as it were a "chorus," but they are far from being a nondescript mass of figures. Each face is summarily but clearly defined, and even when schematically rendered by a few deft touches of the brush, acquires, despite the lack of detail, an individual life.

There is the same diversity in the female figures. In the "pleading woman" turned towards the saint we see sentimental effusion hovering on the brink of tears; the sudden rapture of "the sensitive woman" (a remote recall of certain Baroque retablos) reveals a vast capacity for emotion; while in "the woman in ecstasy" beside her we have what might be an embodiment of maternal love. Most of the women fall into the category of "non-participants," and they illustrate the vast range of variations on this theme that Goya had at his command. Self-satisfied beauty can be seen in the "woman of Algiers" (so reminiscent of Delacroix), vulgar curiosity in the *maja* at her side, while the third young woman in this group, with her sphinx-like smile and huge ear-rings, might personify indifference. The "pretty girl" beside her "supercilious beau" is all gentleness and sweetness, whereas the "mask-faced woman" is a monument of egoism and blind cupidity. Alongside her a woman with a white cloak, her cheek propped by her hand, might be called "the sentimentalist"; and seated near our "toothless beggar" is the "dreamy woman" with a faraway gaze. Goya gives us two quite repulsive versions of old women, on the lines of those in *The Caprices*. One, the old crone with an owlish face and an elaborate chignon, might be a Spanish Mrs Grundy; the other, a fat, sulky-looking hag, is obviously a procuress, a mercenary intriguer of the type embodied by "La Celestina" in the famous novel of that name. Even the small boys have nothing of the innocence of childhood, but the instincts of young anarchists in the making. In short we have here a sampling of the human race, prodigiously varied but everywhere unflattering—the world as Goya saw it!

Very different from this depressing vision of humanity in his depiction of the crowd assembled for the miracle, is Goya's treatment of the angels. Clearly he wished to emphasize the contrast between human ugliness and celestial beauty. It is interesting to find that his imagination, so fertile in its evocations of the diabolic, has led him to portray the denizens of heaven under the aspect of lovely women or innocent little children. These last, however, the luminous, exquisitely rendered cherubs on the intrados and pendentives, were not his own invention, but a legacy from Baroque art. The angels alone are pure Goyesque creations, and it was in the guise of woman's beauty that, at the age of fifty-two, he visualized the joys of heaven. He endowed these youthful forms, elegantly robed in all the sober, harmonious colors of his incomparable palette, with the utmost grace and purity, but always of a wholly mundane order. These charming angels and the little naked children—blissfully unconscious, like the angels, of the iniquities of destiny, man's fate—were all that Goya had to offer by way of uplifting the thoughts of the worshippers in San Antonio, and redeeming the basic pessimism of his message. Yet surely in thus humanizing his angels, he tacitly admitted that sometimes, if but seldom, humanity can shed its ugliness and put on the wings of grace.

Let us then differ from the poet when he writes

> *Painter,*
> *In your immortality Grace weeps*
> *And Horror smiles*[65],

and point out that, if in the cupola of San Antonio horror weeps in Goya's visions of mankind at its most pitiable, grace, anyhow, still smiles in the enchanting angels of La Florida.

GOYA'S FRESCO TECHNIQUE

BY RAMÓN STOLZ

THERE is every reason why the technical procedures, materials and instruments—brushes, spatulas and so forth, not to mention finger-tips—used by great painters have been, and always will be, closely studied by all who are concerned with art, and give rise to heated controversies. The great artist always leaves the imprint of his loftiest aesthetic aspirations plainly visible on even the simplest technical procedure he employs. In his work the balance between inspiration and execution is so perfectly struck that we are inclined to think, often erroneously, that he has had recourse to techniques, materials or tools different from those employed by less gifted men. In point of fact, however, he is subject to exactly the same limitations as any ordinary painter, when he brings off a masterpiece; he uses the same means, including the very simplest. And in the case of Goya and the major work we are dealing with here this is supremely true.

A fresco always reveals clearly and unequivocally the way in which the artist has gone about his work, and, viewed with an understanding eye, has much, sometimes of a surprising order, to tell about its maker's personality. If he is, like Goya, forthright and impetuous, one has a curious impression of watching him at work, standing at his side and even—preposterous though this may sound—acting, in a humble way, as his assistant. For on a close-up view his work comes to life so vividly and so compellingly that—especially if, like the writer, one has spent the greater part of his professional career on scaffoldings with buckets of wet plaster at his side—one seems actually to be standing beside the fresco-painter at that last brief moment of the day's work when the moist, lustrous colors have a beauty and a freshness they will never have again.

In this respect as in many others the San Antonio paintings are a privileged exception; they have kept their pristine freshness and luster to an extent that amazes those who have the advantage of seeing them in close-up, laymen and professional artists alike. But, as it so happens, all this is lost when they are seen from a distance, even with the aid of field-glasses. And here we have an optical phenomenon that at first sight seems inexplicable, especially when we remember that this work is so boldly executed, in large masses, with strong color contrasts.

Like his contemporaries Goya worked in true fresco *(buon fresco)*, not because this permitted a display of virtuosity in a highly exacting technique, but because it is by far the best way of coping with a work of large dimensions. Like Luca Giordano, Tiepolo and Veronese, Goya was perfectly familiar with the oil medium; the reason why he chose the true fresco method was that this seemed to him best suited to the work in hand. Moreover, though some present-day painters seem to take a different view, the fact remains that fresco-painting of this nature offers innumerable possibilities to an artist of an inventive turn of mind.

The raw material of the fresco never changes; it is simple, traditional, and there is not the least mystery about it. What does change from period to period is the manner in which it is handled, the mode of execution varying in accordance with the tastes of schools and individual painters.

None could be better qualified than Goya for handling this medium. We need only refer to that famous work by Palomino, *El museo pictórico*, which has been studied by art students and researchers all the world over. According to Palomino, fresco-painting calls for boldness, vigor and high proficiency in its execution, readiness to take risks, freedom and self-confidence, disdain for over-meticulous procedures, a wholly personal approach. The artist should not come to his work wearied by too much preparation, but in a mood to welcome seeing it grow up under his hands "in a rich impasto unctuous as oils." He must avoid lingering over details (as in the miniature) and rule out stippling. It is important to cover much ground each day, so as to give the work the utmost possible unity. Palomino's dicta were the guiding principles of fresco-painters at the close of the 17th and the beginning of the 18th century, and they were thoroughly in keeping with Goya's own ideas and with his capacities.

The practice of fresco-painting and the special conditions under which the fresco-painter works were bound to have a strong appeal for Goya, given his temperament, and in the frescos in the cathedral of El Pilar at Saragossa and in San Antonio de la Florida we find his idiosyncrasies revealed in the most striking manner, graven as it were in the plaster like the scratches he made when, furious with the drabness of a tone, he scored the painted surface with his nails.

Goya's initiation into fresco took place when at the age of twenty-five he painted the small choir in the cathedral of El Pilar at Saragossa. He had been asked to prove his ability in this technique by painting a fragment, and it met with the committee's approval. In all he painted sixty square yards, according to the measurements made when I was restoring this fresco, and this figure was confirmed by the experts whom I invited to join me on the scaffolding. It was clear that Goya had had little practical experience of fresco-painting at the time, though this work displays all his characteristic verve and resourcefulness. The coarse texture and unevenness of the plaster suggest that Goya laid it himself; it is known that he was required to provide the labor and materials at his own expense. Nowhere did he use tempera, not even for retouching the joins. In one place we can see that he broke off work for the day in the middle of a head and when he started on it again was unable to reproduce the same flesh-tint, with the result that this angel seems to be wearing a mask. He let it stand.

It seems that Goya was obsessed with the idea of what might be called "the enlarged sketch," that is to say adjusting the sketch and its technique to the scale of the final work. This is borne out by his fondness for large masses, the suppression of details, and broad sweeps of the brush. He practises a sort of divisionism in his use of parallel brushstrokes (quite different, be it noted, from hatchings). Using worn, uneven brushes and slashing on his colors at whirlwind speed, he produced a medley of lines giving the effect of an enormously enlarged colored etching. Alternatively we might say that this first work of his is much less like a fresco done in rich impasto than a big watercolor done in dry touches with white patches of the plaster showing through in places. But most interesting, to my mind, are the traces we find here of Goya's recent stay in Italy, the valuable lessons he had learnt in a study of classical Italian painting, lessons which his ready talent was quick to adapt to its own requirements. Here he differed greatly from his fellow artists who, after the customary inspection of the paintings at Herculaneum and the *Aldobrandini Wedding*, came back to make pictures of Iphigenia, Prometheus, or more or less seductive flute-players, so as to keep in line with the neo-classicism which was then the order of the day. Indifferent to subjects that were not contemporary and to people other than those he saw around him, but intensely interested in problems of technique, Goya succeeded, better than any other artist of his time, in taking over all that was finest in the art of antiquity: its austere delicacy of color, its exquisite tonal harmonies, and the grace and suppleness of its brushwork. So thoroughly did he imbibe these qualities that throughout his career this feeling for classical elegance of color and craftsmanship never left him, often checking the extravagances of his wayward imagination and tempering the natural turbulence of his execution with dignity and beauty.

Goya was thirty-four when he started on his next fresco. It, too, was for the cathedral of El Pilar, and its subject was *The Virgin, Queen of Martyrs.* On the previous occasion he had been a beginner, but during the last four years he had been hard at work on his tapestry cartoons and gained much experience. In his frescos in the dome we find the same suavity and limpid coloring as in the cartoons. He averaged five or six square yards daily, the normal rate of progress for a skillful frescoist. He made no use of tempera, even in retouching the joins. His fresco technique is perfect, though unlike that of any other artist and varying even in different portions of his own work.

In fact Goya varied his methods in accordance with the nature of the scene he was engaged on. Thus for the group of white-robed bishops he used the half tone of the intonaco—as a matter of fact the lime has a brownish hue at Saragossa—and probably got his half tints with the dirty water in which he had washed his brushes. Here and there he inserted touches of pure lime to enliven the general effect, while to bring out the bishops' features he added light accents of much-diluted red ochre. This whole scene is bathed in a pearly luster of a singular beauty. Yet the actual painting seems to have been done very rapidly; I doubt if Goya took more than two hours to cover these eight square yards.

But besides these lightning performances, there were others which must have cost him much greater toil and taken a considerable time; where, for instance, he felt that a rich impasto and solidity of color were called for. Finding that the ground of lime, marble dust and pigment did not provide the textural density required, he resorted to a plaster of his own concoction. Applying this to the wall with his hands and working over it with hard-bristled brushes, he got not a smooth but an irregular surface with a low relief or "tooth" on it, which in places reached three-quarters of an inch in height. Upon this rough ground—on which he deliberately left visible the marks of the manipulation it had undergone—he laid in a thick coat of paint, followed up by scumbles, thus obtaining exceptionally vigorous textural effects. The real secret of fresco-painting is that of applying the colors according to the state of the plaster which, after being well soaked when freshly laid, gradually dries off in ten to twelve hours; thus during this time the painter has to work in at least three or four different manners, one after the other. The task of the frescoist who aspires to do more than to take the line of least resistance, that of spreading flat color over the spaces enclosed within the contour-lines incised on the wall, calls for much resourcefulness. He has not only the ordinary problems of the painter to contend with, but has to fight against time as well. When I examined these frescos in close-up, I was amazed by Goya's ingenuity in coping with these difficulties.

Bearing in mind the fact that these paintings were to be seen from a considerable distance, he troubled little about absolute accuracy in the drawing or in details of faces and figures. Not unnaturally those who examined them from near by were horrified, and jumped to the conclusion that this was the work of an irresponsible dauber. That anyhow was the impression it produced on Goya's brother-in-law Francisco Bayeu, who was "artistic adviser" to the committee in charge of the decorations in El Pilar. Bayeu was no less quick-tempered than Goya and there was a stormy scene between the two men. Work was stopped then and there and the dispute dragged on for over three months. Goya ended up by falling out with everyone, not only with the Building Committee and the cathedral Chapter but even with his friends at Saragossa, which was practically his hometown.

Seventeen years later he was asked to decorate the church of San Antonio de la Florida. This time he had a free hand; Bayeu had died and there was no one to prevent his painting the frescos exactly as he pleased. The cupola (nineteen feet in diameter) was not large; the scaffolding provided seems to have been a good one, and in no way cramped his movements, judging from the amount of wall surface he was able to cover in a single day's work. Goya was now fifty-two years old; he had completely mastered the fresco technique, was bursting with ideas and energy and delighted to be working independently at a task that was thoroughly congenial.

Circumstances being so propitious all around, the San Antonio frescos shaped up from the start as a prodigious compendium of everything Goya had done before and at the same time anticipated, to a quite remarkable degree, the masterpieces of his old age, including the "black paintings." He threw himself into the work with such exuberant self-confidence, and such serene disregard of what any of his predecessors had done in the same field, that beside these paintings even the boldest, most brilliant creations of all those who came after him look like the ventures of timid amateurs.

He painted again in the traditional fresco technique, as he had done twice before. But now for the first time he went to considerable trouble in coping with one of the chief inconveniences of fresco-painting. I refer to the "joints" inevitably left in both the paint and the plaster at the end of each day's work. The point is that, since the paint must be applied while the plaster is still wet, the artist only lays on as much plaster as he can paint within the day. When he stops work any plaster left unpainted is cut away up to the edge of the surface already painted. Next day fresh plaster is laid on the succeeding stretch of wall and the work of painting continues. The result is that a joint or seam is left between any two portions of the wall painted on successive days and this the artist is obliged to obliterate as neatly as possible *a secco*, generally in tempera. Furthermore, several colors brilliant in hue—vermilion, for example—fail to resist the decomposing action of wet lime plaster and therefore were applied in tempera after the wall surface was quite dry. The same is true of certain blues, which Goya put on only in light, glancing touches, never with slow, deliberate strokes of the brush.

As usual with Goya, guide-lines sharply incised in the freshly laid plaster were enough to give him his bearings for the day's work; they established the scale and general lay-out, leaving all details to be settled later. In our photographs these lines are plainly visible. But Goya was not the man to follow them blindly. He was the creative painter *par excellence*; it was his way to improvise as he went along, to act on each flash of inspiration and on the spur of the moment. So it is that at many places the finished figures no longer bear the slightest relation to the incised preliminary design, which Goya, characteristically enough, did not even take the trouble to efface.

As against this, however, it seems clear that before starting work he decided exactly what colors he would use (their range was always limited) and in what order they were to be applied. Similarly, though a figure in its final form might differ from the initial conception, the entire technical procedure behind it had been thought out beforehand.

It is a noteworthy feature of fresco-painting that the colors can be laid on in broad sweeps of the brush without concealing the preliminary design, since it is incised in the raw plaster. The choice of the ground tints is a matter of prime importance, for even when they have been worked over with the darker and lighter shades of each pigment, they determine not only the predominating tone of grey but also the values of all other colors. In all the paintings of antiquity the artist generally began by laying in greenish greys as a foundation for the flesh-tints and everything not requiring strongly characterized colors. The range of greens used went from Verona terre verte to the greenish hues produced by ochre, black and lime. Frescoists were not alone in employing this procedure; it has been clearly detected in unfinished works painted in other techniques. Goya's innovation at San Antonio was his use of black and the greys obtained from black mixed with lime as the ground colors of his fresco. On to these he applied a mixture of lime and marble dust pure or tinted as seemed suitable, leaving the flesh-parts untouched for the moment and bringing out volumes. According as he loaded his impasto with brighter tones, worked over it and diluted it, the pearly grey ground-color shot with gleams of pink, violet and yellow took on a rich variety of hues and textural effects.

Upon this lustrous texture of tinted greys he rubbed light scumbles which "took" on the lime of the underlying colors. For these finishing touches he confined himself almost exclusively to iron oxides, to earth pigments of various hues from vivid reds to yellow ochres, and greens and blues used sparingly to brighten up the work as a whole. At many points, especially on the brilliant ochres of the curtains, these scumbles give the impression of having been painted at the end of the working day when the plaster had dried and would no longer absorb the paints. Given not only these scumbles, but the retouchings in tempera of the joins between portions of the wall painted on successive days, and the additional fact that with the passing years and seasonal variations of temperature and humidity the plaster tends to crumble—given all this, it must be admitted, I feel, that there was some justification for the widespread belief that Goya employed a mixed technique of fresco and tempera for these paintings. The truth is, of course, that a painter as accomplished as Goya was, capable of bringing a figure to life with a few bold strokes of the brush, had no difficulty in meeting the demands of true fresco painting. What is more, the very dexterity and rapidity with which he worked are quite out of keeping with a mixed technique. In fact the retouchings in tempera of the various joints, especially those beneath the cupola, are so painstakingly made that I am inclined to regard them as the one part of the work where Goya may have had the help of an assistant. Only the practising frescoist can appreciate how maddeningly laborious such retouches can be—unless recourse is had to hatchings. Until the San Antonio frescos Goya never touched up the seams between portions covered in successive days. But the use of tempera for these indispensable retouchings is one thing; a "mixed technique" is quite another matter.

Given the sobriety of the colors and the simple methods employed, Goya was not held up by problems of execution and could impart their utmost dynamism to the forms and colors on the wall surface. When there is talk of Goya's "secret," all this amounts to is a recognition of his vast talent as a painter. It is amazing to see how much he simplified his procedures, so as to be able to work in perfect freedom and with the maximum efficacy; he always forged unswervingly ahead, making light of obstacles. And that was the path he took, once again, at San Antonio de la Florida.

Nevertheless, many theories have been put forward as to the technique Goya used in painting the San Antonio frescos. I will cite only one of them—not with any polemical intent—, that which the eminent Spanish critic Aureliano de Beruete published in 1915. According to him, the "secret" of the execution consisted in Goya's use of sponges instead of brushes for putting on the color. This insistence on a specific tool rather than on more painterly considerations was quite in the spirit of the time when Beruete advanced this theory; hence its prompt success. Even today there are many who regard the technical procedures of the great masters as highly skillful studio recipes, tricks of the trade in short. And the discovery of a tool which might explain "how it was done" is a godsend for those who think on these lines. The oddest thing of all is that Beruete lit on this explanation not after examining the frescos themselves in close-up, but from a study of the colorman's bill. Much has been said and written about this famous statement of account which, including the hire

of the carriage which took Goya to and from his work, adds up to the grand total of 14,314 reals, a small fortune in those days. This is not the place to go into the exact use he made of those 342 lbs of pigment, including 1000 reals' worth of vermilion, and over ten dozen brushes. But one item, that of 70 reals' worth of sponges, calls for comment. They were employed (as they still are) to clean the exceptionally large palette used by fresco-painters —on this point we need only refer to Palomino—and for no other purpose. Their use for purposes of stumping is confined to watercolor, and ruled out in fresco-painting since, if dabbed on to wet plaster, sponges would leave streaks, besides removing some of the intonaco. (They are used in this way by stucco-workers for simulating marble.)

Beruete is equally mistaken when he suggests that most of the work was painted in tempera in which glue-water was the vehicle with which the pigments were bound (hence, he says, the twelve reals' worth of glue in the colorman's account). But nobody in that day used glue-water for painting on dry plaster composed of lime and sand. The media used were milk, the yolk and white of egg, or casein, or a mixture of all three, these agglutinants being the vehicles that take best on this kind of support. All practising artists, even the veriest tyro, knew this. Yet Beruete writes: "We need only examine the patches of color representing the embroidery and ornaments of curtains serving as a background to the figures, to see that these cannot have been done in oils or *a fresco*, since in that case the individual brushstrokes could not have been so clearly marked as they are here. The only possible explanation of this effect is that the artist painted in tempera or watercolor and, since watercolor is ruled out for obvious reasons, it follows that Goya must have made use of tempera." Anyone who has done fresco painting and studied frescos in close-up will find Beruete's argument hard to follow. I would go farther and say it is so preposterous that no practising painter can take it seriously. In both fresco and tempera painting water is the diluent and these two techniques are so closely allied that to distinguish between brush-strokes made in one or the other is out of the question. The truth is that, ever since the mid-19th century, when fresco-painting came to be regarded as a sort of "occult technique," the mystery of mysteries, the most absurd opinions have been expressed about it. Needless to say, none of the theorists responsible for these absurdities had ever handled lime, even for whitewashing a wall. Our photographs of details taken in a slanting light give a good idea of the superb brushwork of the great artist who made these frescos. For anyone who can appreciate richness of texture, the "feel" of a surface, these photographs are more revealing than any technical description. Beruete, like all who had seen these paintings at a distance, was led into a series of mistakes because lime has a slow and steady action on ferric colors, the effect of which is to raise their tone. This is why haematite (iron oxide red), whose natural hue is blood-color, as the name suggests, turns carmine after a certain time. Whereas no change takes place in greys composed of black and lime. The greater the distance from which one sees them, the more leaden and phosphorescent they appear, tending to overpower and darken the adjacent colors. But on a close view this optical phenomenon ceases to operate and we see the colors in all their richness. The greys are there simply to make the other colors "sing," and it is as if a veil were being lifted from before our eyes when we approach the frescos. But until now only a privileged few had been able to enjoy the wonderful effect produced by these paintings in close-up—an experience in which, thanks to our color plates, the public can now share.

NOTES

PAGE 14

[1] This tapestry cartoon, now in the Prado (No. 788), dates from 1780. There is a smaller version of the same theme in a Swedish collection.

[2] Prado, No. 786. Painted in 1779.

[3] The first place of worship at the Gate of San Vicente, an open shed, is said to have been donated by one Pedro Arias, a pious Catholic who placed in it a statue of the Virgin of Grace which had been brought to Spain by Calced Augustinian friars. On Arias' death the toll-house officers took over the little shrine, to which mud walls had now been added. Villanueva's effigy of St Anthony—he made a replica of it for the convent of Tiemblo—was inspired by a picture by Pedro de Valpuesta. These data (and some set forth on a later page) are taken from a record drawn up, it seems, for the information of the Patriarch of the Indies, and containing a résumé of the history of the churches of San Antonio de la Florida. Dated 1804, this document is signed by a priest of the name of Antonio López Figueroa. According to Pascual Madoz' *Diccionario geográfico, estadístico y histórico de España y sus posesiones de Ultramar* (Madrid, 1848-1850), the church built by Churriguera had stucco ornaments on the inner walls, a type of decoration which appears to have been characteristic of Madrilenian Baroque.

[4] La Florida and La Moncloa are names still used to designate the stretch of land extending from the Montaña del Príncipe Pío to the Puerta de Hierro which now stands at the junction of the Pardo and Corunna roads. La Moncloa, which I can remember as having been a charming, little frequented park, is now the site of university buildings. It was here that a famous rake in the days of Philip IV, the Marquis of Eliche, once resided. Reconstructed and embellished by successive owners, his house had developed into a small, exquisitely proportioned, neo-classical palazzo by the time it came into the possession of the Duchess of Arcos and her daughter Doña Cayetana, later Duchess of Alba. Unfortunately the small Palace of La Moncloa, as it was usually called, was destroyed during the Civil War of 1936-1939. Rebuilt recently at public expense, it is now a museum containing works of art from the collections of the Kings of Spain. Further information regarding its history can be found in Joaquín Ezquerra del Bayo's *El Palacete de la Moncloa*, Sociedad Amigos del Arte, Madrid, 1929.

[5] *Topografía de la Villa de Madrid descrita por Don Pedro Teixera el año 1656.* An excellent facsimile was published by the Municipality of Madrid some years ago, when this plan of the city, accompanied by an erudite commentary, was reproduced in *Guía de Madrid para el año 1656. Publícala 270 años más tarde Don Luis Martínez Kleiser*, Madrid, 1929. The section of the map including La Florida and La Moncloa (No. LXXVII) shows the La Florida gardens with all details clearly indicated: fountains, groves, flowerbeds and the hermitage (i.e. that of "The Virgin of Grace").

PAGE 15

[6] The purchase (or exchange) of land east of the Pardo road, of the Paso Viejo estate owned by the Hieronymite Order, of the Almendros gardens owned by the Count of Noblejas, and of the Marchioness González de Castejón's grounds (formerly the Botanical Gardens) took place in 1795. In 1796 the king acquired by exchange the so-called Belén estate and bought a strip of land at Cantarranas from the Duke of Alba. This information is derived from the File marked "La Florida No. 1" in the Royal Archives, Madrid. See also Joaquín Ezquerra del Bayo's *El Palacete de la Moncloa*, Madrid, 1929.

[7] Cf. Javier Marquina, *Compañía de los Caminos de Hierro del Norte de España... Historia, actuación, concesiones, etc.*, vol. I, pp. 30 and 54, Madrid, 1940.

[8] This document, inscribed "Aranjuez, May 16, 1792," begins: "In order to carry out the works for which the king has given verbal instructions, on the estates and plots of land in the Montaña del Príncipe Pío which have been acquired, His Majesty desires you to enter into negotiations with the Monastery of San Jerónimo, Madrid, with a view to purchasing at its proper value the land within the Huerta (orchard) facing the Fountain of El Abanico, owned by the said monastery, and all the land needful for erecting on this site the new chapel of San Antonio, in replacement of the ancient church of La Florida. This latter is now to be pulled down as a preliminary to starting work on the new building for which the king has given orders."

[9] *Las Iglesias del antiguo Madrid*, vol. I, pp. 119 and 207.

[10] He was given a fixed salary by the king, as from 1789. His post at the Buen Retiro had previously been filled by Don Santiago Pavía and Santiago Bonavera el Viejo, who was succeeded by his cousin Santiago Bonavera el Mozo in 1772; on the latter's death in 1790 Fontana succeeded to the post. The records disclose that he lived in the Real Sitio del Retiro and had a carriage of his own.

[11] I recall having seen it stated in print some years ago that the present church of San Antonio de la Florida was the work of the architect Juan de Villanueva. Neither Llaguno nor Ceán Bermúdez in his *Noticias de los arquitectos y arquitectura de España* mentions Fontana; he is not cited as a painter in Ceán Bermúdez' *Diccionario histórico de los más ilustres profesores de las Bellas Artes en España* (1800), nor in Thieme-Becker's *Allgemeines Künstler-Lexikon* (1907 etc.). Records relating to the church name Francisco Ribas and Carlos Chornet as foremen, Don Bernardo Potoc as quantity-surveyor, and Juan Antonio Bermejo as overseer. I have studied the contractor's accounts; these are passed and signed by Fontana for the years 1792-1793, 1793-1794 and 1795-1796. In 1792 monthly payments of 50,000 reals were made for the work in progress; this was reduced

to 25,000 reals on March 1, 1793. Fontana must have been fairly old at the time; in 1796 he complains in his reports of bad health and failing eyesight, due apparently to a stroke. In 1797 he sought the king's permission to go to Archena and Valencia to take the waters; thereafter no further mention is made of him in any extant records.

PAGE 16

[12] Mass was said for the last time in the old church on July 10, 1792 (according to Antonio López Figueroa).

[13] The title is even longer and continues: *Con un elogio de la nueva estatua del Santo hecho por el profesor Don José Ginés. Añádese un resumen de la vida de este glorioso confesor y sus gozos. Dedicado a los fieles ministros del Resguardo de la Renta de Madrid y de todo el Reino. La saca a luz con motivo de la nueva capilla que la piedad de nuestro católico monarca (que Dios guarde) ha mandado erigir a este gran santo, un devoto suyo.* I have inspected the copy that once belonged to the Royal Library, quoted by Tormo in his *Iglesias del antiguo Madrid*; it is a pamphlet of 44 pages printed by José Herrera at Madrid in 1798. It contains a summary of the history of the hermitage and by and large corresponds to the account given by López Figueroa (cited above). But the author makes the mistake of giving Churriguera's Christian name as Juan, Villanueva's as José, and Fontana's as Francisco. He praises to the skies the statues made by Villanueva and Ginés, but never so much as mentions Goya's name. This curious omission can be accounted for if we assume that the pamphlet went to press before Goya had been commissioned to make the frescos, so that it might be published in time for the opening of the church (which in the event was postponed for a year). This would also explain why the author omitted to specify the exact dates in his text —so as not to delay publication of his pamphlet. The effect is odd to say the least of it. Thus we read: *This new chapel of San Antonio, the third, was completed in the present year 179..; a new statue of the saint, nowise inferior to its predecessor, has been placed within, and its beauties will be revealed to the public on the ... day of the month of ..., 179... It was made by that exceptionally able professor of art, Don José Ginés.*

The pamphlet ends with a eulogy in verse of which the following is a literal prose translation:

"Raise, Manzanares, your forehead bulrush-crowned, and if my song delights you, stay your humble course between your golden banks. While until now you owed your felicity to the famous chapel, built by Christian piety upon your shore and dedicated to the miracle-worker of Madrid, surely henceforth you will flow more joyfully, now that mirrored in your foaming stream another church has arisen on your eastern bank, built by Fontana at the King's command. It was the Corinthian Order that he chose, for its opulence, its beauty, and its aptness to the interior of the church; or else because of its heaven-aspiring valor. Need we be astonished by the noble art with which this Italian designed the Paduan's church, when King Charles's generosity gave his hand total freedom? And what wonder he endowed it with such lavish beauty when in the King's devotion to the Saint he had a model of supreme perfection!"

At the end of the poem is an envoy in eight lines addressed to the king, a gem of that contemporary pedantry which reveled in mythological allusions. The poet hails the king in the first line as the "Spanish Alcides" (Hercules) and two lines later likens him to "a stalwart 'atlas' upholding two worlds" (the old and the new). The final couplet runs: "Image and chapel will bear testimony / To thy devotion to Saint Anthony."

[14] The Count of La Viñaza, in *Goya, su tiempo, su vida, sus obras* (Madrid, 1887), gives the date as July 1st.

PAGE 17

[15] These biographical notes were published by Beroqui in *Archivo Español de Arte y Arqueología*, 1927.

[16] As regards Carderera, see my study, *La situación y la estela del arte de Goya (Antecedentes, coincidencias y influencias del arte de Goya)*, Madrid, 1947, page 24. In the article he published in *El Artista* (1835) and also in that in the *Semanario Pintoresco* (1838), Carderera makes special mention of the San Antonio frescos.

[17] The information which I owe to the courtesy of Don Federico Navarro and Señorita Junquera, who were kind enough to make researches in the archives of the Royal Palace, throws no light on the original order for the San Antonio paintings or the payments made to Goya. Even Sambricio, in the numerous records he has published in his *Tapices de Goya* (Madrid, 1946), where much is said of Goya's dealings with the Court, has nothing new to give us as regards La Florida apart from the facts contained in the invoice recorded here (note 18).

[18] The public records office of the Royal Palace, Madrid, informs me that the original statement of account is no longer to be found either in the La Florida file or amongst any of the papers relating to La Florida. The whereabouts of the original being unknown, we must here content ourselves with giving an English version of the statement as recorded by the Count of La Viñaza in his *Goya, su tiempo, su vida, sus obras* (Madrid, 1887), in which it reads as follows:

Statement of account for painting materials and other articles delivered by the druggist Manuel Ezquerra y Trápaga to Don Francisco de Goya for the decoration of the church of San Antonio de la Florida.
Madrid, December 20, 1798.

Archives of the Royal Palace
Patrimonies, Royal Domain of La Florida
File no. 1.

Statement of account of painting materials and other articles which I, Don Manuel Ezquerra y Trápaga, tradesman domiciled in this Court, have delivered to Don Francisco Goya, King's Painter to His Catholic Majesty (may God preserve him), for the work in the chapel of San Antonio de la Florida, which he carried out at His Majesty's bidding in this year, 1798, invoice itemized as follows, errors and omissions excepted:

Firstly, June 15, 1798

Item	Reals
One half arroba of light ochre	12.17
One half arroba of dark ochre	25
One half arroba of fine ground crimson, at 10 reals per lb	125
One half arroba of black earth, at 8 reals per lb	100
One half arroba of enamel, at 10 reals per lb	125
One half arroba of red earth	12.17
One half arroba of Venetian umber . .	50
One half arroba of fine green clay at 16 reals per lb	200
Eight lbs of fine light yellow at 16 reals per lb	128
Twelve and a half lbs of Chinese vermilion from the Real Estanco at 80 reals per lb	1000
One half ream of large-size imperial paper	250
Eighteen large earthenware pots for the colors at 8 reals per pot	144

The 26th of the same month

Item	Reals
Fifteen lbs of red earth	15
Ten lbs of dark ochre	20

The 5th of July

Item	Reals
Five dozen Lyons brushes, large size, at 5 reals each	330
Twelve fine-haired brushes of different sizes, at 20 reals each	240
Two large brushes, letter K, with ferrule	30
Two ditto, letter E	12
Four lbs of glue	12

The 30th of the same month

Item	Reals
One half arroba of light ochre	12.17
One half arroba of dark ochre	25
One half arroba of fine crimson, at 10 reals per lb	125
One half arroba of black earth, at 8 reals per lb	100
Two and a half arrobas of smalt, at 10 reals per lb	625
One half arroba of red earth	12.17
One half arroba of fine umber	50
One half arroba of green clay, at 16 reals per lb	200
One half arroba of minium	50
One half ream of imperial paper . . .	250
Eight lbs of light yellow	128
One and three-quarters lbs of fine washed sponges, at 40 reals per lb	70
One dozen fine-haired brushes, at 20 reals each	240
Three containers for calcining the colors	9

The 11th of August

Item	Reals
One hundred and sixty reals for the purchase of pots and basins	160
Nineteen and a half lbs of fine ivory black, at 24 reals per lb	468
Four lbs of flower of indigo, at 64 reals per lb	226
For twenty-two lbs of ground Molina blue, at 15 reals per lb	330
Four lbs of Sienna earth	128
One and a half lbs of superfine London carmine, at 40 reals per ounce . . .	960
One half ream of imperial Genoa paper, large size, to the value of 250 reals	250

The 26th of the same month

Item	Reals
Two dozen fine badger-hair brushes . .	240
Three lbs of English blue	78
One dozen badger-hair brushes	96

The 22nd of October

Item	Reals
Two ounces of superfine lake, at 200 reals per ounce	400
One lb of lamp-black	10
And for the expenses of a carriage hired to convey Don Francisco Goya from his home to the church of San Antonio and back, I have paid six thousand two hundred and forty reals at the rate of fifty-two reals per day every day from August 1 to the completion of the work.	6,240
	14,314

Grand total: fourteen thousand three hundred and fourteen reals. Madrid, December 20, 1798 = Manuel Ezquerra y Trápaga. Approved = Francisco de Goya. Passed = Florencio Martínez. Received = Trápaga.

[19] Our information regarding Goya's illness and the form it took leaves much to be desired. We know that he had his first attack at Cadiz at the end of 1792; he became deaf, his sight was impaired and he had difficulty in keeping his equilibrium. He also became paralysed and it took him some months to recover the use of his limbs. Work was out of the question and some time elapsed before he could take up his brushes again. Contemporary records give the impression that he had a relapse in 1794, but we know that by this time he was busy painting again; only his hearing showed no improvement, and in fact he never recovered it. The best description of his illness can be found in Sánchez Cantón's *Vida y obras de Goya*, Madrid, 1951.

PAGE 21

[20] See the photograph published by Garnelo in his book *La ermita de San Antonio de la Florida y las pinturas de Goya*, Madrid, 1928.

PAGE 22

[21] This monument, a sort of cylindrical cippus—hence the curving surface of the inscribed stone—, marked the place where Goya lay, beside Goicoechea, his son's father-in-law, in the cemetery of the Grande Chartreuse of Bordeaux. A photograph of this, Goya's first tomb, is included in Manuel Mesonero Romanos' little book *Goya, Moratín, Meléndez Valdés y Donoso Cortés. Reseña histórica de los anteriores enterramientos...*, Madrid, 1900. The Latin epitaph was written by Don José Pío de Molina, a Spanish émigré and one of Goya's friends at Bordeaux. Pío de Molina's was the last portrait he painted before his death. The inscription, it will be noticed, contains a double error: Goya died in April, not May, and at the age of 82, not 85.

PAGE 23

[22] For example in Goya's picture of San Bernardino of Siena preaching in the presence of King Alfonso V, in the Church of San Francisco el Grande, Madrid. For further information on this point see my article *Sobre el cuadro de San Francisco el Grande y las Ideas estéticas de Goya,* in *Revista de Ideas Estéticas,* Madrid, 1946.

PAGE 24

[23] As is well known, it was Goya himself who coined this phrase. In the biographical notice given by the painter's son Xavier to Don Valentin de Carderera, we find the following remark: "His best pictures clearly prove that he had mastered all the problems of the art of painting and was an adept in—to use an expression often on his lips—'the magic of the ambiance' of a picture." See in this connection *Archivo Español de Arte y Arqueología,* Madrid, 1927, and my article cited above *Sobre el cuadro de San Francisco el Grande,* first published in *Revista de Ideas Estéticas* (1946) and reprinted as an appendix to my study *La situación y la estela del arte de Goya* (1947).

PAGE 25

[24] *Goya en zig-zag,* Madrid, 1928, page 78. "We might exclude from Goya's work all his murals, with the exception of the 'black paintings'... yet the solid rock of his personality would remain unshaken, intact; nothing that matters would be lost." To Encina's thinking, San Antonio and the paintings in it are "a mere fantasy"!

PAGE 27

[25] Readers of these pages should bear in mind the fact that the church points almost due north. It is on the north side of the cupola that the scene of the saint and the dead man recalled to life is painted.

PAGE 28

[26] On the other hand, this figure is wholly true to life. As Rothe says, "It is exactly the same type of monk as we see nowadays getting on to any Spanish train."

PAGE 92

[27] For the information of readers interested in this sequence, I may refer them, as regards the paintings in the lower portion of the Church, to the most fully documented book on the subject, previous to this one, which contains a series of photographs in black and white taken by the Madrid photographer Moreno. This book, entitled *Iglesia de San Antonio de la Florida, Madrid, Pinturas de Goya,* has not been widely circulated; it comprises Vol. IV of *Biblioteca selecta del Arte español,* published in 1924 and edited by Don Manuel Vega y March.

PAGE 105

[28] Mayer assumes that Goya started painting on June 15, the date on which the first batch of supplies was delivered, but it is clear that actually he started work at a later date.

PAGE 106

[29] The notes on Goya by Father López were published in full in La Viñaza, op. cit., page 465. Professor Stolz discusses them in his study *Las pinturas al fresco del templo del Pilar,* published in the Saragossa review *Aragón,* March-April, 1942, pp. 32-41.

[30] Sánchez Cantón has unearthed a curious entry in Moratín's *Journal,* published in his *Obras póstumas* (Madrid, 1867-1868), vol. III, p. 255, and relating to approximately this date. It runs: "With Goya at San Plácido. Looked at the paintings." Sánchez Cantón's apt assumption is that Goya made the round of the churches of Madrid which, like San Plácido, are decorated with frescos, with a view to clearing up his ideas on the subject. As a result of this inspection, he decided to exclude Baroque forms more and more from his work.

[31] This sketch figured in the Centenary Exhibition organized by the Prado in 1928. See the *Catálogo ilustrado...,* compiled by me, item No. 40, p. 42. It measures 10¼ by 15 inches. The study was naturally made on a flat surface and once Goya started work on the curving wall of the cupola, he realized the problem set him as regards the scale of his figures and the great modifications this necessitated. The same problem came up as regards the sketch made for the apse. This second sketch has the same dimensions, and figures in the *Catálogo ilustrado* as No. 41, p. 43.

PAGE 107

[32] Mayer, *Francisco de Goya,* Madrid, 1925 (Spanish edition), Nos. 11 and 13 of his catalogue. Sánchez Cantón, in his *Vida y obras de Goya,* confesses that he, too, has no knowledge of them.

[33] Rothe, op. cit., plates 6, 7 and 8. These are very skillful pen drawings, similar to many others by Lucas in which he reproduces or imitates Goyesque subjects with much ease and elegance of line. Some are interesting variants of Goya originals. Four are reproduced in my *La situación y la estela del arte de Goya,* plates 55-58. Quite recently some other small pictures, which, it is suggested, may be preliminary sketches for San Antonio, have been published. But the technique and quality of these works, judging by the reproductions, make me question their attribution to Goya.

PAGE 108

[34] See note 5 in the *Catalogue of an Exhibition of Spanish Paintings,* The Metropolitan Museum of Art, New York, 1928.

[35] See Ossorio y Bernard, *Galería biográfica de artistas españoles del siglo XIX,* 2nd edition, 1883-1884, p. 314.

[36] This is why this very fine picture has been dated to about 1798. For more about Asensio Juliá, see my book *La situación y la estela del arte de Goya,* pp. 152-154 and 362.

[37] No. 326 in his catalogue of Goya's works.

PAGE 110

[38] See my book *La situación y la estela del arte de Goya*, Madrid, 1947.

PAGE 111

[39] See his study *Los fondos de Goya*, Madrid, 1946.

[40] Oscar Hagen, *Patterns and Principles of Spanish Art*, Madison (Wisconsin), 1948.

PAGE 114

[41] I doubt if any contemporary work exists (none has in any case been published) in which reference is made to the La Florida paintings; nor was anything said about them by Goya's writer friends. Perhaps such of them as saw these paintings regarded them as mere diversions of no great significance.

[42] Eugenio d'Ors, *El vivir de Goya*, in *Epos de los destinos*, pp. 166-167.

[43] J. López Rey, *A Contribution to the Study of Goya's Art. The San Antonio de la Florida Frescoes*, in *Gazette des Beaux-Arts*, New York, April 1944. This study was published in Spanish in *Goya y el mundo a su alrededor*, Buenos Aires, 1947.

[44] Palomino's description of "the colors specially suitable for fresco-painting" runs: "These are all natural mineral colors, some of them in the raw state, some calcined or otherwise submitted to the action of fire. Native mineral pigments are: light and dark ochre, red earth, crimson, reddish brown, Venetian umber, rosso antico, terre-verte and black earth; those submitted to the action of fire are: enamel blue, charcoal black, burnt ochre, light yellow, burnt vitriol (copper sulphate) and vermilion, though this last is better in the raw state." Palomino, book 7, chapter V.

PAGE 116

[45] Professor Stolz was able to study the paintings very thoroughly when a scaffolding was erected with a view to cleaning them after the end of the civil war; he had another opportunity of examining them in 1955 when the photographs were taken for the present book. On this occasion he was instructed by the Academy of San Fernando to carry out a restoration in the top of the cupola where a small leak had developed.

[46] In this connection readers may consult the report made by Venturini-Paperi, the painter who in 1914-1916 restored Correggio's frescos in the dome of Parma Cathedral. It was published by Corrado Ricci in his *Corrège*, Paris, 1930, pp. 164-166. Correggio kept to the *buon fresco* technique but with the addition of retouchings, where he thought fit, in transparent washes and tempera.

PAGE 118

[47] See chapter III on the problem of Goya's early training in my book *La situación y la estela del arte de Goya*, Madrid, 1947.

PAGE 120

[48] *La pintura al fresco del templo del Pilar*, in the periodical *Aragón*, Saragossa, March-April, 1942.

[49] Built in the year 1770 on the initiative and at the expense of an Aragonese nobleman, the Count of Ricla, viceroy of Catalonia.

[50] Due probably to the good offices of the Saragossan businessman Don Juan Martín Goicoechea, Goya's loyal friend and patron. Doubtless Goicoechea commended the young painter to the architect. Documents relating to the commission given Goya for the frescos in the *coreto* were published by the Count of La Viñaza, op. cit., pp. 157-159. They were also dealt with at length in Pascual Galindo's article *Goya pintando en el Pilar* in *Aragón*, pp. 152-158, April, 1928.

[51] The sketch is in a private collection in Saragossa. It was published by Sánchez Cantón as plate 1 in his *Vida y Obras de Goya*, Madrid, 1951.

PAGE 123

[52] For a fully documented account of this incident see La Viñaza, op. cit., pp. 162-167, and Galindo's article in *Aragón*, April, 1928.

[53] Acquired in 1805 along with some sketches by Bayeu from the collection of Doña Angeles Sulpice Chopinot. According to an inventory compiled by Jacinto Gómez, King's Painter and decorator of the side-altars in La Florida, this lady owned fourteeen pictures by Goya: studies of bulls, shipwrecks, attacks by brigands, a fire, etc. No doubt she was a local collector who liked Goya's work and had been one of his earliest patrons. See Galindo's article in *Aragón*, April, 1928.

PAGE 124

[54] Much the same garment, virtually the standard uniform of Goya's angels, is worn by the angel in *The Annunciation* (1785) in the Osuna Collection.

[55] The fresco representing *The Virgin, Queen of Martyrs* was extensively restored by Stolz fifteen years ago. It was in very bad condition, subsidences having taken place due to the inadequate foundations of the church, which was built on the bank of the river Ebro. Some of the cracks were so big, Stolz told me, that he could put his arm into them.

PAGE 125

[56] César Pemán, *Los Goyas de Cadiz*, Cadiz, 1928.

PAGE 126

[57] In the article *Merveilles enfouies*, published in the *Figaro Littéraire*, Paris, December 27, 1953.

PAGE 127

[58] F. J. Sánchez Cantón, *Como vivía Goya*, Madrid, 1946.

PAGE 128

[59] Goya lived at Bordeaux with Doña Leocadia Zorrilla, who was separated from her husband Don Isidoro Weiss, a businessman of German origin. Before this they had lived together in Madrid and most of his contemporaries believed him to be the father of Doña Leocadia's daughter, Rosarito.

PAGE 129

[60] True to his principles, Goicoechea had emigrated to Bordeaux. It would seem that he had held an important post at Madrid under Joseph Bonaparte. He died at Bordeaux on July 2, 1825.

[61] I have in mind a shrewd appreciation of Goya contained in an article published in French in 1835. It figures in a review, signed *Ad. M.*, of a book of "impressions of Spain" by Alexander Slidell, an officer in the United States Navy. Goya is referred to as an artist whose works are little known, a sort of "Spanish Rabelais." The writer stresses the social and anticlerical aspects of Goya's art, and shows an acquaintance with *The Caprices*, probably the only work by Goya he had seen. Cf. the appendix of my book *La situación y la estela del arte de Goya*, pp. 301-302.

[62] Galván's etchings were exhibited, and awarded a second prize, at the National Exhibition of 1878 at Madrid. The very fine artist's proofs which figured there are now in the National Library, Madrid. They are much superior in quality to the edition, on large paper, which was published in Madrid ten years later with a foreword by Don Juan de Dios de la Rada y Delgado, entitled *Frescos de Goya en la iglesia de San Antonio de la Florida grabados al aguafuerte por José María Galván y Candela...* Rada y Delgado's introduction makes it clear how little interest was felt in the La Florida paintings at the time; at one point he refers to them as "these almost forgotten frescos."

PAGE 130

[63] A long, detailed and well documented "solution" of the mystery is to be found in José Almoina's *La póstuma peripecia de Goya*, Imprenta Universitaria, Mexico City, 1949.

This is the gist of what its author has to say on the subject. As regards the disappearance of Goya's skull, the commonly accepted view was that most probably a phrenologist had got hold of it for purposes of study. But it is most unlikely that Goya's family, who attended the funeral, would have allowed a doctor to desecrate the body in this manner. Thus, though the coffin showed no sign of having been broken open, it must be assumed that the theft took place at a later date. In 1849 a Spanish artist Dionisio Fierros (1827-1894) painted a picture (now in Saragossa Museum) representing a skull; on the back of the canvas can be read—or anyhow could be read some years ago—an inscription: "Goya's skull, painted by Fierros." One of the painter's descendants, Dionisio Gamallo Fierros, has given an ingenious, if somewhat unlikely explanation of what happened. According to him the skull was made over to the son of the Marquis of San Adrián, whose portrait Goya painted in 1804, and it was in the Marquis' home at Tudela that Fierros painted it, and it subsequently was given to him. The skull, Gamallo says, remained in his grandmother's possession until about 1910, when it was broken up by someone who was studying anatomy and knew nothing of its history. All the fragments were dispersed except two, which he still possesses. See Gamallo's article in the newspaper *El Español*, Madrid, February 20, 1943.

[64] Though the perils to which the frescos were exposed in a church that was in constant use for public worship were fully recognized, long negotiations were needed before their safety could be ensured. The first thing was to have the church classified as an "historic building," and the Academy, not without difficulty, got this done in 1905. In 1909 a committee of academicians was appointed to look into the conditions under which the services were conducted in the church and the damage caused to the frescos, and to submit a report to the authorities. Their report *Estado de las pinturas de la iglesia de San Antonio de la Florida* was published in the 1910 Bulletin of the Royal Academy of San Fernando, pp. 49-52. The matter was dealt with again in the 1911 Bulletin (p. 39), in which stress was laid on the necessity of building another church for the use of the parishioners. Some years later (in 1915) the minister concerned called for a report on the then condition of the frescos, and the committee accordingly drew up a statement entitled *Informe acerca del procedimiento empleado por Don Francisco Goya en las pinturas decorativas de San Antonio de la Florida.* Though this report, as can be gathered from its title, deals with the "procedures employed by Goya," we have not alluded to it in the body of this book, for the good reason that the committee were given no opportunity of having a close-up view of the frescos, and thus the statements in the report as regards the technique employed were, admittedly, mere conjectures. The project of building a new church near the old one and exactly like it took form in 1918, and funds were raised by public subscription, contributions being made by the Municipality of Madrid, the Council General and the Government. In 1926 the Municipality made over for this purpose the land it owned beside the old church. A well-known writer and corresponding member of the Academy, Don Ignacio Bauer, took an active part in raising funds for the building of the new San Antonio and in 1925, with this in mind, published a brochure (now become a collector's item) entitled *En el nombre de Goya*, illustrated with drawings by Ricardo Marín. On May 14, 1928, the king signed the deed of transfer of the church of San Antonio to the Royal Academy of San Fernando, one of the conditions being that the church should henceforth bear the name "Hermitage of San Antonio de la Florida and Pantheon of Goya." A résumé of the various steps taken to obtain this result will be found in the Proceedings of the Royal Academy of San Fernando of 1927-1928, pp. 28 et seq.

PAGE 133

[65] Rafael Alberti in his poem *A la pintura*, Buenos Aires, 1948.

INDEX OF NAMES

TABLE OF CONTENTS

INDEX

CONTENTS

THIS VOLUME OF THE COLLECTION

PAINTING ◦ COLOR ◦ HISTORY

WAS PRINTED

BOTH TEXT AND COLOR PLATES

BY THE

SKIRA

COLOR STUDIO

AT IMPRIMERIES RÉUNIES S. A. LAUSANNE

FINISHED THE THIRTY-FIRST DAY OF OCTOBER NINETEEN HUNDRED

AND FIFTY-FIVE

PRINTED IN SWITZERLAND